Ronnie and Hilda's Romance

Ronnie and Hilda cutting the cake on their wedding day, 21st June 1947.

Ronnie and Hilda's Romance

TOWARDS A NEW LIFE AFTER WORLD WAR II

WENDY WILLIAMS

Matador
9 Priory Business Park,
Wistow Road, Kibworth Beauchamp,
Leicestershire. LE8 0RX
Tel: 0116 279 2299
Email: books@troubador.co.uk
Web: www.troubador.co.uk/matador
Twitter: @matadorbooks

ISBN 978 1789017 977

British Library Cataloguing in Publication Data.
A catalogue record for this book is available from the British Library.

Printed and bound by CPI Group (UK) Ltd, Croydon, CR0 4YY
Typeset in 11pt Adobe Caslon Pro by Troubador Publishing Ltd, Leicester, UK

Matador is an imprint of Troubador Publishing Ltd.

For Ronnie and Hilda: this is, after all, your story.

INTRODUCTION

Ronnie Williams and Hilda Cartwright met by chance one day in November 1945, and at that moment their lives changed forever. This book is the story of what happened to them in the following eighteen months, in the aftermath of the Second World War which had ended only weeks before. During that year and a half, whilst circumstances forced them apart, they wrote to each other every couple of days, leaving a fascinating portrayal of what life was like for a young man still abroad in the army, and a young woman starting her career as a teacher and coping with the shortages and deprivations of a Britain struggling to return to normality.

Although both their families were based in Rochdale, Lancashire, their backgrounds were very different. There are some gaps in information about Ronnie's father, Thomas Henry Williams, from Blaenau Ffestiniog in North Wales. He claimed to have been born in 1863, but because there was such a very large difference in age between him and Ronnie's mother, he may have shaved a couple of years off his true age, and really have been born even earlier than that. Ronnie believed his father may have had a previous marriage, that his wife was an alcoholic, and that Ronnie may have had half-brothers and half-sisters he never knew. What is certain is that by the time Ronnie was born, his father had done quite well for himself working in the cotton industry in Manchester, and was fairly well-off. It is not known how he met Ronnie's mother, Ethel Wall, born in 1890 at Didsbury, near Manchester.

Ethel had a younger sister, Minnie, to whom she was very close, and who looked very much like her. Their father, William Wall, made his living out of horses: he was at various times a coachman and an ostler, and he gave private riding lessons. He was therefore not a wealthy man, and it is a mystery how the family managed to pay for Ethel to become a student at Rochdale College of Art, where she painted and drew the forms considered acceptable for women at the time, i.e. still life, architectural studies, wallpaper designs, animals and plants. She was very talented, won competitions at national level, and became a qualified art teacher.

There is no evidence that Ethel and Ronnie's father, known as Harry, were actually ever married, and possibly he had never been divorced from his first wife. Whatever the case, they lived together as man and wife from the early 1920s onwards. Ronnie's sister Hettie was born in Derbyshire (from where Harry commuted to work in Manchester) on 17th February 1923. Perhaps as an accident of birth, she was never quite normal, and at the time people would have said that she was "a bit simple". It must therefore have been a great relief when Ronald Henry Williams was born, a year later to within a day, on 16th February 1924, at a lovely house, Lark Hill, in New Mills, Derbyshire, and was a perfectly healthy baby.

In 1926, Minnie emigrated to Australia with her husband, who was a chemist. They took with them Ethel and Minnie's by then widowed and retired father. Although they corresponded regularly until Ethel's death (Minnie lived for quite a few years longer than Ethel), they never saw each other again. In fact they never even spoke, since Ethel never had a telephone. She had therefore already lost one of her main sources of companionship and support.

In Ronnie's first five years, they had a comfortable life, with a car and a servant, and he and Hettie had very desirable toys: Ronnie had a beautiful reproduction Bullnose Morris car he could sit in, with all the accessories, and Hettie had a very fine toy pram.

The difference in age between Ronnie's parents, and the fact they may not have been married, probably did not matter too much whilst they were financially secure, but then in 1929 disaster struck. Ronnie's father lost all his money very suddenly in the Depression, and they instantly became poverty-stricken. Despite Ethel's art qualifications, it was not considered acceptable for married (or apparently married) women to work outside the home, and they lived on the point of starvation from then onwards.

Harry eventually found some work as a door-to-door salesman, and, according to Ronnie, people could not believe he was so poor because he was so well-dressed, still wearing his bowler hat. It is certainly from his father that Ronnie got his love of having a smart appearance, and of discipline. With Harry's paltry income, the family lived from hand to mouth for the next five years, often going hungry, and on one occasion being evicted for not being able to pay the rent. Ronnie's toy car had to be sold; not surprisingly, he cried. On one occasion, all he got for Christmas was an orange.

Just when it seemed as though things could not get worse, Harry died of a cerebral haemorrhage, when Ronnie was just ten; he was by then in his seventies, and worn out with the hardship of the family's life. Shortly before he died, he represented himself at a court case in Manchester against a major textile company which owed him some money. He won the case, and after his death Ethel used most of the money for a grave and headstone for him in Rochdale Cemetery.

Needless to say, things then grew even worse for Ethel, Ronnie and Hettie. Ethel got a strong letter of recommendation from the vicar at Rochdale Parish Church, as she applied for menial jobs, such as assistant to the caretaker at Rochdale Girls' High School, and Ronnie was sent away for almost four years as a boarder to the Bluecoat School in Oldham. At the time, the school specialised in taking in boys who had lost one or both parents, and financially this was a godsend for Ethel. Conditions were extremely harsh: Ronnie used to say it was like being in a borstal! Any boy found wearing a vest in bed, no matter how bitterly cold it might be, would be caned, for instance, and the school day would start with running and/or swimming before breakfast, no matter what the weather.

Nevertheless, Ronnie received a good education whilst he was there, there were some teachers he was fond of, including one known as "Pop" Bond, and the school had a trip to London in 1936, so it was not always unbearable. Above all, it taught him to look after himself and stand up for himself, and furthered his love of neatness and self-discipline which was to stand him in such good stead in the army.

When she was fourteen, Hettie left school to start work as an operator in a textile factory which made items such as dusters: it was the only type of job she could ever cope with, and she remained in that same job, remarkably, until she was fifty-nine. Ronnie also left school to start work on his fourteenth birthday, in the drawing office at Thomas Robinson's, an engineering company in Rochdale. His wage at the time for a full working week, plus Saturday mornings, was 10s., in other words 50p.

Ronnie was intelligent, articulate and a quick learner. His spelling was virtually perfect, and he was always an excellent organiser. He would have flourished if he had been allowed to continue his education, but his mother desperately needed the money. Unfortunately, the fact of starting work when he was so young meant that he never had any formal qualifications, and that was to prove an obstacle to getting promotion or a better job in later years.

He was glad to be back home, but there was never any money for entertainment, and sport was his only outlet in his spare time. When war broke out in 1939, he was still only fifteen, and obviously too young to be conscripted. However, as soon as he became sixteen, he joined the main Home Guard in Rochdale, and as well as working full-time he was soon regularly on firefighting duty at night, learning how to use weapons and throw Mills grenades. Like his time at the Bluecoat School, this experience was also invaluable to him when he enlisted in the army in 1942, aged eighteen. An indication of how poor Ronnie's family was, and how badly nourished he was, is that when he joined the army he was really quite underweight. He was fairly tall, 5 ft 10 ½ in. (he would later grow to be 6 ft) but weighed only 9 st, and had a 34 in. chest.[1]

Ronnie had no idea where he would be posted when he was sent abroad, but he devised a very clever way of letting his mother know, when he wrote his censored letters home. Before he left England, he looked up all the places where combat was taking place and thought up a code name for each country, that is, a personal name with the same initial letter as the country. For example if he wrote home: "I have seen George", that would mean he was in Gibraltar.

In many ways he was mature, tough and experienced for his age, but in others very innocent: although he was sensitive, kind, good-looking, and, all his life, an emotional person, he had never had a girlfriend. He had simply never had the opportunity.

After some initial training in Britain, Ronnie was assigned to the Royal Artillery, then spent almost all of the next five years, which should have been the best years of his life, fighting abroad, and, when the war was over, keeping the peace for eighteen

---

1 According to the printed information in Hilda's diary for 1946, the average height for Englishmen then was 5 ft 7 ½ in, and the average weight was 11 st 1 lb, which shows just how undernourished Ronnie was for his height.

months. He was sent from Gibraltar to North Africa, then to Italy, and became a bombardier. He was eventually transferred to the Loyal North Lancashire Regiment because they needed reinforcements. He took part in some major battles such as Cassino and Monte Grande, as the Germans were gradually driven back by the Allies. After Mussolini and his mistress were executed, Ronnie saw them hanging upside down in the square in Milan.

When the war ended, Ronnie was still posted in Italy, and was still only twenty-one. He had seen sights and experienced things that no one should have to undergo, yet he was one of the rare soldiers who felt able to talk about his experiences. He was never afraid to show his feelings, and in later life often cried when he told how his friends had died, sometimes in his arms; or how he had seen a soldier have his head blown off and still keep on running for a few paces; how he himself had missed being hit by a bullet in the head by just an inch when he rose up too high from a trench; how he had endured, in turn, scorching heat in Gibraltar and Africa, freezing cold in Italy, hunger, sleeping on ground cloths, marching for miles carrying heavy kit, as his regiment gradually moved up Italy. He did not get any leave between 1942 when he was conscripted, and 1945 when the war ended.

In other words, when Ronnie met Hilda at the end of 1945, since the age of five he had had a very hard life by anyone's standards. She, on the other hand, had been far more fortunate. Her parents came from very humble origins, but by dint of sheer hard work they managed to create security, and a happy and largely carefree life for Hilda.

Hilda's father, Wilfred James Cartwright, was born in 1896 in Ludlow, Shropshire. Ludlow is a beautiful town with some wonderful old buildings and is deservedly a very popular tourist location these days. Although only small, it has over 500 listed buildings, and in 1943 John Betjeman called it "probably the loveliest town in England". However, when Wilfred was born there was some terrible poverty, since most work was based on agriculture, which was both seasonal and dependent on climatic conditions. It is clear that his parents, William and Eliza, always struggled to make ends meet. Illness and insanitary conditions were rife: people even caught typhoid from drinking polluted water. Altogether the couple had fourteen children, starting with Mabel in 1891 and ending with Charlie in 1913. Only five of them survived to adulthood, and out of those only three lived to old age. One of Wilfred's brothers, George, burnt to death as a toddler in 1902 when his nightshirt caught fire from a spark from the hearth; the tragedy was reported in the *Ludlow Advertiser*. William Cartwright, and in turn Wilfred, took absolutely any work available. At various times William had been a coachman, a gardener and an agricultural worker. By the time Wilfred was fifteen, for example, they were both working in a quarry. But eventually the work dried up altogether and the family was forced to move to Birmingham just before the First World War.

When war broke out, Charlie was a baby and Wilfred, the only other surviving male offspring, was just the right age to be conscripted. One can only imagine what anguish his parents must have felt at having to let him go off to battle in France, with the Royal Warwickshire Regiment. However, unlike so many other young men, Wilfred was "lucky". He was not killed, but injured by shrapnel, and survived. He was sent to recuperate to Stubley Hall, a "big house" which had been requisitioned, between Rochdale and Littleborough, and it was there that he would meet his future wife, Edith Ashworth, who lived nearby, whilst he was still wearing his "hospital blues", the uniform worn by injured soldiers. Fate seems to have taken a hand, since they would certainly never have met under normal circumstances.

Halifax Road is the main road between Rochdale and Littleborough. Smallbridge is halfway between the two, and going in the direction of Littleborough the little districts merge seamlessly into Hurstead, Smithy Bridge, Dearnley, Stubley and Featherstall, then into the town of Littleborough. The family of Hilda's mother, Edith, had lived in one or other of these places for generations. Edith's maternal grandfather, Robert Whipp, was an engineer, first in a colliery and then in a cotton mill, and it was always felt that Edith's mother, Emma, had married beneath her station when she wed Edmund Ashworth, who appears to have been illiterate, and always had manual jobs, often as a labourer. It was said that Emma's father belonged to the family which ran the local engineering company Whipp & Bourne, in existence for many years until early in the twenty-first century. Emma and Edmund had seven children, five of whom survived, and Edith, born in 1897, was the youngest of them. Of her surviving siblings, her sisters Clara and Emily and her brother Willie worked in Hurstead Mill, where Edith would also work, but her other brother Josiah, known as Jesse, two years older than her, had serious epilepsy, then considered something of a stigma, and could not get a job at the mill, not least because he would not have been safe near the machinery. Eventually, he started working as a rag-and-bone man, with a horse and cart.

As was the case for Wilfred's family, in Edith's parents' household every penny counted. When she was a young girl, Edith used to be sent to the pub on Friday night to make sure her father came home before he could spend all his wages on drink. Edith used to tell that she and Jesse would have to share an egg between them because there was so little money available.

Edith had to start work at the mill part-time when she was twelve, beginning at six in the morning, and if she fell asleep in the afternoon at school she would be caned. She started work full-time in 1910 when she was thirteen as a "frame back tenter". Clara and Emily, thirteen and eleven years older than Edith respectively, had by then left home to get married, Willie was a "spinner" and her father was a "scavenger" for the Urban

District Council (presumably this involved some form of waste or rubbish collection).

Tragedy would strike the family repeatedly in later years: Willie was killed in the First World War – he was a bandsman – leaving two very young children behind, Jesse died of heart failure in 1934, aged only thirty-nine, and Clara, depressed and having been left by her husband, committed suicide in 1937 by putting her head in a gas oven. So, from then onwards, only Edith and Emily were left.

After Edith and Wilfred met, and he was discharged from the army with a very small pension (he never regained full use of one hand), he went back to live at his parents' house in Birmingham and to work in a rubber factory nearby, but he and Edith carried on meeting, and they finally married in 1920. They lived with Edith's mother, Emma (her father had already died by then), and looked after her in her final years when she "took to her bed" and died in 1928. Wilfred continued to do any kind of work he could find, including at one stage working for a cobbler, briefly working in the employment exchange itself, and finally getting a job in a bakery in 1923. He would continue to work there, doing a night shift in the bakery, until 1950.

Edith and Wilfred had a baby, Harry, who died when only a few weeks old, in 1922. Their only surviving child, Hilda Edith Cartwright, was born on 4th August 1924. Edith would become pregnant again subsequently, but lose the baby when almost at full term.

From the outset, although to begin with money was short, Hilda had a healthy, happy and stable childhood, playing with her older cousins Bill, who was the son of Emily, and Marjorie, the daughter of Clara. As children did at the time, she played out in the street, was allowed to sit on her Uncle Jesse's pony, named Jewel, and got told off from time to time for wandering off down the tramlines with the dog when she was very little, or falling in a nearby pond when she stepped onto the ice. She always did have an adventurous streak! She was considered to be a clever girl, and having attended the same primary school as Edith, that is Saint Andrew's at Dearnley, she won a full scholarship to Bury Grammar School.

When she was twelve, in 1936, Edith achieved her girlhood dream of getting a shop, a grocer's and off-licence, at Smallbridge, again on Halifax Road, and the business did well. By 1945 Edith and Wilfred were able to buy the premises, and obviously as part of a package, three small cottages nearby. Hilda had a problem-free adolescence, and, with the exception of any national shortages, really never lacked for anything. Her parents bought her a piano (she had lessons at school), she joined the Guides affiliated with the Methodist Church at Dearnley (she was brought up as a Methodist despite going to a C of E primary school) and enjoyed various sports, and the family had enough money to go out for meals, to the cinema, and on excursions to the seaside, usually to Lytham St Annes or Morecambe, often taking Marjorie with them. The only restriction was that someone always had to be there to look after the shop.

Even during the war, Hilda did not suffer unduly: because they had the shop they always had enough to eat, and even had fresh eggs from the hens which Wilfred kept. She sat her school-leaving exams, known as Higher School Certificate at the time, in 1943 when she was seventeen, and again won a scholarship, to teacher training college. She should have gone to Leeds, but the college was evacuated to Scarborough for the entire two years of her training, and all the students were put up in quite a high-class hotel, where their meals were served to them. Postage was so cheap that she used to send parcels of laundry home to be washed and have them posted back again. She had, of course, the benefit of sea air, a good social life with friends from the college, and not very serious boyfriends from amongst all the many servicemen stationed nearby. For the rest of her life she loved going back to Scarborough because of the happy times she had had there.

So Hilda was a fully qualified teacher by the time she was nineteen, and was in her second year of teaching at Elm Street Secondary Modern School in Middleton, still living at home, when she and Ronnie met for the first time.

Again, it seemed to be fate that they met: as Hilda says in one of her letters, they could so easily have missed one another. At the time, Bill and his family (wife, Annie, and young daughter, Susan) had a bathroom, whereas Hilda's parents still did not, and, quite simply, Hilda went to visit them to have a bath. When she emerged from the bathroom, there was Ronnie, who had come to see Bill, a former work colleague of his. Ronnie was home on his first leave since he joined the army.

It was clear that Hilda and Ronnie got on very well on that occasion, but Ronnie was too shy and inexperienced to ask Hilda out. So Bill fixed them up with each other: he told each that the other wanted to go out on a date together. Ronnie was back in England only for a short time before being sent back to Italy and then on to Austria, no longer fighting, but keeping the peace and on guard duty. Indeed, they got on so well, and in view of the uncertainties of Ronnie's situation in the future, he proposed to her after they had known each other for just ten days. They were sitting on a bus on the way to Manchester at the time. He could only afford to buy a ring with the tiniest of stones, but she treasured it more than words could say. Only a few days after that, Ronnie had to go back abroad, and their long period of separation started.

They began to write to each other immediately, at least every couple of days for the next eighteen months, knowing sometimes that the letters would not arrive for a long time, and in one case, with no address to write to. In January 1947, Hilda received letters from Ronnie, but since he did not know at that point where he was going to be posted next, he was unable to give her an address where she could write back, and she had written seventeen letters by the time she was able to send them to him. On one occasion, it was again another whole six months before he got any leave. The letters are one of the ways in which they got to know each other, and in them they both show remarkable strength of character and wisdom for their age, bearing in mind that they were both twenty-one when they met, and that Ronnie was only twenty-three, and Hilda twenty-two, when they got married.

What they wrote gives a fascinating and detailed picture of what life was like at the time. Hilda had her job and quite a good social life: she was able to go to evening classes, out to the cinema and plays, to go away on holiday and on courses, but she was still subject to the shortages, strikes and vicissitudes experienced by everyone in Britain at that time. Ronnie was promoted at an astonishing rate, and was a staff sergeant, the highest rank of a non-commissioned officer, by the time he was twenty-two. But even though the war was over, he was still undergoing dreadful hardship, often cold and hungry, under orders to shoot escaped prisoners and looters, attending war tribunals, and trying to keep his own men in order.

The letters speak for themselves. They show the couple's fears and emotions, strengths and weaknesses of character. Ronnie is remarkably perceptive in his views of people and situations, Hilda shares the humour of dealing with not very bright children at school, and when things go wrong during building work at home. Even she has her distressing times, such as when her dog is killed.

It is thanks to Ronnie's meticulousness in dating every one of his own letters, and writing to Hilda: "Thank you for your letters of 10th February, 12th February and 14th February", for example, that it has been possible to put their respective letters in the order in which they would have been read, rather than in the order in which they were sent. The countless endearments, the thousands of kisses, have been omitted, as has anything which is intensely personal. Those matters remain theirs, and theirs alone.

Ronnie's Background

One of Ethel's watercolour paintings from her days as a student at Rochdale College of Art. According to the label attached to it, this was part of a set commended in a national art competition in 1911.

Ronnie's parents, Harry and Ethel, with baby Hettie in 1924. Ronnie's mother was expecting him at the time.

Hettie, Ethel and Ronnie in 1928: Ethel's bohemian dress was made of purple velvet. Ronnie remembered this, and said how much he loved the dress, right until the end of his life.

Ronnie, aged five, in his beloved reproduction Morris car.

Ronnie on a school trip to London in 1937 from the Bluecoat School. He is second from the right on the front row, and already impeccably smart. This was apparently in relation to the coronation of George VI.

Ronnie's identity card for Thomas Robinson's, when he was fifteen.

Ronnie's enlistment details, showing just how malnourished he was; that did not stop him from being recruited into the army.

A very accurate sketch drawn of Ronnie by a street artist in Milan, shortly before the end of the war. The picture took only twenty minutes to do.

Hilda's Background

*Edith's mother,
Emma Ashworth,
in Edwardian times.*

*Wilfred in his
"Hospital Blues" during his
convalescence at Stubley Hall.*

Edith aged twenty in 1917, at the time when she met Wilfred.

Hilda and Bill in 1930: Bill was always her protector.

A scene from Hilda's happy childhood. Emily, Edith and Hilda at "Scenic Studio, Pleasureland, Southport".

*Hilda's piano, bought by her parents in 1936, and still in use now.
As well as family photographs, the picture shows the clock awarded
to Wilfred by his workmates at Henry Whittle's bakery when he
retired from there in 1950, after twenty-seven years' service.*

*Ludlow in 1937, the
same summer Wilfred
took Hilda there to
help her get over the
tragedy of her friend's
drowning. At the back
Wilfred's youngest
brother, Charlie, their
parents, Eliza and
William Cartwright,
and on the right
Eliza's sister, Jinnie.
Iris is at the front.*

Marjorie, Wilfred and Hilda in Blackpool in Hilda's youth. The Tower can just be seen in the background.

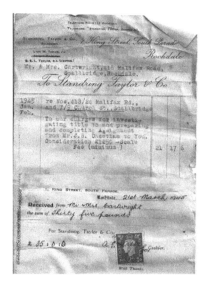

The amounts Wilfred and Edith paid for their properties in Smallbridge in 1945.

Hilda in 1945, shortly before she met Ronnie.

Ronnie & Hilda's letters,
December 1945 – April 1947

Hilda's letters for the first six months of their correspondence are missing. Ronnie took them home in the summer of 1946 to his mother's home, and they were subsequently lost. However, much of what she must have written was clear from what he said in his replies.

Pte R.H. Williams
"C" Coy 2ⁿᵈ Loyals
C.M.F.[1]

8.12.45.

I've very little time to write this letter as the train which I'm travelling in is moving off in twenty minutes. This is my first chance I've had to write to you, and believe me it is a great relief to be able to do so. When I write to you, I feel as though I'm

---

1   The addresses and/or rank are given here on the letters only when they change. Earlier, during the war, Ronnie had been in the Royal Artillery, where he had gradually risen to become a bombardier. When he was transferred to the Loyal North Lancashire Regiment he had to start again from scratch as a private, but was very quickly promoted.

nearer to you. As you know, I went on the 2.15 from Manchester arriving at Euston 7 p.m. and then it was just one mad rush through the Tube to Victoria, London. I've never seen so many troops on that station in all my life: the train to Folkestone was due out at 9.30 but did not depart until 11.15 so you can tell how many troops there were. We arrived at Folkestone 12.50 and at 1.30 a.m. went across to Calais, arriving there at 3.25. It was terribly rough, and plenty of blokes were sick (I wasn't). I was really browned off at Calais because we were messed about for three and a half hours, first in one room to get blankets and then signing papers left and right. We got ninety cigarettes and a bar of chocolate. Everything seemed to be going wrong, kit bags flying all over the place. We left Calais 6.30 a.m. on Thursday and stopped twice for food. Thursday night we passed through Paris and slept that night as well as we could with eight in a carriage. Friday morning we stayed half an hour in Switzerland, it was snowing heavily, and now it is 10.30 a.m. Saturday morning and I'm starting this letter in the train. This place is called Domodossola and is just on the Italian border, so we expect to be at Milan sometime Sunday morning. I shall be glad when I get back to my unit and settle down. I've been thinking of you all the time. I told the lads I got engaged and they said, "Good old Ronnie, but you certainly shock us". They liked your photos too. It's a goods train, there are no lights in, but I can just see what I'm writing by the light of a candle. I will write again as soon as I get the opportunity.[2]

---

2   This was Ronnie's return to his regiment after meeting Hilda and getting engaged: one can only imagine the trauma of having to separate after having known each other for such a short time. The journey from Manchester to Milan appears to have taken four days.

10.12.45.

Forgive me if you cannot understand my writing, my hands are so cold I can hardly keep hold of my pen. I thought it was cold in Blighty, but it's nothing to this weather. It snowed a little yesterday, but I think it would be warmer if it snowed heavily. I'm now back with the dear old Loyals, but not at the prison camp. Some artillery unit took over about three weeks ago. I'm writing this letter in barracks, which is miles from nowhere and looks more like Belsen. We are about twelve miles from Milan. I've made a good start on my return as I'm on guard tonight for twenty-four hours and then tomorrow we move to a hospital near Milan where we do more guard duty, so really, we are no better off than at the prison camp except perhaps conditions are a little better. This battalion has fifteen different places to guard in and around Milan, although one company is training French troops on British weapons. We get very little time off, but when I do, I spend it writing to you and sleeping.

We have such a lot to look forward to; what a beautiful wife I will have. I wonder what it will be like when you have a baby. I'll be rushing home from work, doing the housework, making the bed, and even doing Monday's washing and ironing. Oh yes, I can wash clothes. That's one thing the army has taught me because we have to do our own.

By the way, I've got a lovely cold. I'm really enjoying my eyes watering because I caught it off you!

I must close now, it's 4.45 p.m. and I'm on guard at 5 p.m. I'll think of you tonight and every night I'm on guard.

PS I enclose a photo of baby Ronnie[3]: keep it for our family album, we can show it to the children one day.

---

3   The photograph of Ronnie in his toy Bullnose Morris car when he was five, as shown in the illustrations.

13.12.45.

I've done nothing but guard duty these last few days in hospitals, patrol points, salvage dumps, etc. In the salvage dumps there are thousands of tyres, and as I told you, the Italians give anything to get hold of them. The other day we shot thirty-one Italians trying to get these tyres. Now the guards are doubled.

The food is terrible so far. This morning for breakfast we had powdered egg and that was all. The bloke who invented that stuff ought to be shot. To think if I were at your house tonight, I'd be having pie and chips![4]

I'm writing this letter in a village on the outskirts of Trieste: we came up here yesterday to take some Jerries back to Milan. It's quite a large convoy. When I get back to Milan, I suppose I'll be doing more guard duty.

I've been thinking of you all the time. Remember that joint bus ticket? Well, I was only looking at it today, and what memories it brought back to me. The 1st December, 2.15 p.m.[5], and I must not forget the 918 bus. I've been terribly quiet since I got back. The fellows see me sitting quietly, and say "Never mind, Ronnie, she's thinking of you too".

Some of the lads have scrounged some wood and have made a nice fire as it's terribly cold outside. It's a barn we're sleeping in tonight. I shouldn't be surprised if there is no barn in the morning; it will probably be burned down.

By the time you get this letter you will have had your hair done: keep it nice for me, I'm sure you will.

God bless you and all at home.

---

4 From the fish and chip shop just across the road from the grocery and off-licence owned by Hilda's parents in Smallbridge, where they went once a week.

5 The moment when Ronnie proposed to Hilda.

16.12.45.

As I write this letter my hands are freezing: I'm writing this letter in bed or in between my three blankets and they are about as thick as the *News of the World* but I'm certainly glad of them. The bed is just about holding me up; I suppose I'm lucky to have one. I remember this time last year I was at the infantry training depot lying on a mud floor, a few weeks later I was in the line and crouching in a slit trench, but those days are gone and I never look back, but what a different outlook I have this year from last.

I saw a football match yesterday at the Milan stadium. That was my first day off since I left home. The teams were Naples and Florence, and what a match it was, ripping shirts off each other's back and fighting. Naples won by three goals to one. The crowd was in a lively mood because as the teams went off the field the Naples supporters attacked the Florence team so the Florence supporters joined in with a lovely free-for-all. There must have been 2,000 people having a go and the police hadn't a chance but that's just like the Italians. I got out of the stadium in double time; I want to get home the same way as I left. While I was in Milan, I got you some snaps of the place[6], also of Rome and Venice, but I'll send them on later.

I would like to have been with you all at Christmas, but never mind, this time next year I hope to have finished with the army and be with you for always.

At present we're guarding a supply depot in Milan. It's terribly cold at night on guard. We're supposed to patrol the place but despite all the amount of patrolling I do all the stuff could be taken and I wouldn't know. I make a fire and sit by it. I'll be thinking of you at night school tomorrow night. By the time you

---

6   As shown in the appended photographs, together with Ronnie's and Hilda's letters.

get this letter it will be Christmas, so I'll take this opportunity of wishing you a very happy Christmas and to all at home, I'll be thinking of you, have a good time, you deserve all the best.

19.12.45.

I'm writing this in the guard room, 2 a.m. Wednesday morning. I've just come off guard and don't feel very tired so I thought I'd write to you. I'm on guard again at 6 a.m. so I'll go to bed when I've finished this.

It's a fortnight today since I last saw you. Remember a fortnight last Monday we saw Bob Hope in *Princess and the Pirate*? The mobile cinema came here last night with that film. I only saw a bit of it because I was on guard, but all the time I sat there I was thinking of you. I'll be thinking of you tomorrow night finishing school for the Christmas holidays. How nice it would have been had I been with you and what a wonderful time we'd have had.

I wrote to one of my pals at Robinson's at 10 o'clock at night and told him what a lucky guy I was. I suppose the news will soon spread, I want all the world to know. I've no news except I'm still guarding Italy. God bless you, I'll write again soon.

25.12.45.

Thank you for your three letters which arrived yesterday; you can imagine how happy I was when I knew they were from you.

Well, it's Christmas Day, 10.20 a.m., and here I am writing this crouched in the back of a wagon 200 miles from Florence on the main *autostrada*. We've stopped for fifty minutes and I thought I'd better write and tell you how much I love you. We stopped in a small town yesterday and that's when I got your letters. The mail had just arrived at the army post office; a few minutes later it would probably have been sent to the Loyals in Milan and I'd have had to wait until I got back. So far, the journey has been wicked – due mostly to the weather. It's done nothing but rain for seven days and as I write this the rain is just rolling off the roof of our wagon, snow is everywhere and my poor fingers are dropping off. The driver has been cursing all the journey saying it's just like the army to do this job at Christmas time. We should arrive at our destination this afternoon and set off back sometime tomorrow. During one of our stops yesterday I called in at the mobile laundry and had a lovely shower. I'll be thinking of you tonight at Bill's, I do hope you enjoy yourself. I wonder what Susan's face was like when she knew Father Christmas had brought her a car. Won't it be nice when we can tell our children about Father Christmas? This is just like any other day to me – for breakfast this morning I had corned beef and biscuits.

I'm pleased to know you called to see Mother, I'm sure she was glad to see you. What did she think of the ring? I can't tell you what it's like to plan our future. I never thought I'd meet the right girl so soon.

I didn't think you had a fortnight's holiday for Christmas. It seems years since I went to school, perhaps that's the reason I'd forgotten how long the holiday was. It's a nice change for you and you'll be able to do some of your jobs at home and see more of your friends.

I wish you a very Happy New Year: remember me to all at home.

27.12.45.

We arrived at the destination 2.30 p.m. Christmas Day. It was dark about 4.30 p.m. and the billet we slept in for the night hadn't a single light or bulb in the place. We had no candles, so you can imagine what a stew we were in. I struck five boxes of matches in an attempt at sorting my bed out, and we were all in bed by 7 p.m. What a time to go to bed on Christmas Day. It must have been 12 o'clock before I got to sleep. Before that, I was thinking of you and all the wonderful times we had together.

I'm writing this sitting in the front of the wagon and we're going fifty miles an hour down this lovely smooth road. This is going to be short because we're only twenty miles from the army post office, and I wasn't going to wait until I got back to the Loyals before I wrote to you. I always write even if I've only a few minutes; after all, you come before everything now.

I do hope you enjoyed Christmas Day at Bill's, although I suppose it was quiet. You are never out of my thoughts.

L/Cpl. R.H. Williams
"C" Coy 2nd Loyals
C.M.F.

30.12.45.

At long last I'm back with the Loyals and what a time we've had to get back. We were 350 miles from Milan and nothing but mountains all round us when our wagon broke down, and there wasn't a wagon with a tow rope. That was 8.30 a.m. It was 10 p.m. before a wagon came to tow us back. It's a good thing we had some food or we would have been without all that time. What made me feel mad was our own kit was on one of the front wagons. If I'd had the kit, I could have written to you but instead I sat there thinking of you and looking at your photos. I arrived back about 6 a.m. this morning, had some breakfast – porridge (like sawdust) and powdered egg – what a breakfast!

I didn't go to bed as I'd so many jobs to do; the first one was my washing. I'd quite a pile too. I've hung it up to dry but heaven knows when it will dry because it's like an ice box in this place. For my next job I scrubbed my equipment then polished brasses and, the best job of all, I made my bed, so you see what a mix-up I've been in these last few days.

Once again, I'm an NCO. When I arrived back from that wonderful leave a CSM asked me to do some clerical work for the RSM. I saw the RSM and he said, "I'd like you to have this job because your place is an NCO". I certainly wasn't going to refuse it for two reasons; one because I like responsibility, and two because being an NCO is more money on my gratuities when I leave the army, and we need all the money we can get, don't we? However, they've caught me for duties already. I'm on staff parade tonight. It's just checking a nominal roll of the company and pulling the flag down. I hope I'm not boring you with this army routine, but it's just to let you know what I'm doing.

When I got back there was your letter dated 19th December waiting for me. Thank you, I do look forward to them. I'm sorry you lost all that wage for the few days you had off school, but it was worth every moment of it, wasn't it? But I think you've got some brilliant ideas for colour schemes; perhaps that's a ladies' privilege.[7]

A month ago today you saw my mother for the first time. I suppose you'll be seeing a lot more of her, I know she likes seeing you.

I'll say goodbye for now but I'll write again soon, remember me to your mother and father. Look after yourself and God bless.

---

7   Hilda was by this time in her second year as a teacher at Elm Street Secondary Modern School in Middleton, a few miles from home. Clearly, she thought it worthwhile to ask for unpaid leave for the precious few days she had with Ronnie before he went back. She has obviously already started planning what their home together will be like.

1.1.46.

A very happy New Year and lots of luck and happiness! I'm orderly corporal tonight, so I haven't much time to write this.

I spent a night in Milan last night, the second time out since I arrived back from leave. I went to La Scala Opera House to see *Madam Butterfly*. It was very good, but I didn't understand it at all. That is when I miss you more than ever when I'm walking round the city. Since I've been orderly corporal my job has been mostly chasing blokes around for guard or marching the defaulters to and from their meals or making out company orders which usually read: *reveille 6.15 hours, breakfast 7.00 hours, parade 8.00 hours. Kits to be laid out on the bed by 9.00 hours smart and in a uniform manner, brasses on all equipment will be highly polished. Anyone caught failing to comply with these orders will be subject to severe disciplinary action...* And that is what our company orders are every night, plus a few extra details like fatigues, etc. It's just like being at school where you're told what to do.[8]

Are you receiving my letters? I haven't had a letter from you for eight days now. Everyone is the same, there are none coming at all; I suppose the weather is the answer.

Just before I started this letter, I was sewing buttons on my shirts and darning socks, polishing brasses, cleaning my rifle and a whole lot of little jobs.

Perhaps at this moment you're in London with Mash.[9] Wherever you are, enjoy yourself.

---

8   Being smart was extremely important to Ronnie, all his life. During the war he was frequently selected as the "Stick Man" for being the smartest person on parade. On one occasion the choice was between him and another soldier, and he lost because he had one stud missing from underneath one boot. He used to manage to get knife-edge creases on his trousers by putting them under his groundsheet and sleeping on them overnight.

9   This was the nickname of one of Hilda's friends from teacher training college, made up from her initials, Marjorie A. Stephenson-Holland.

The Italians were going mad in Milan last night celebrating New Year's Eve, singing, dancing, and sending off rockets and fireworks. Some of the blokes said that the noise during the early hours of the morning sounded as though the guns were firing in Anzio, but for all the noise it didn't waken me. It certainly feels nice to have a few nights in bed instead of on guard.

4.1.46.

It's 10.30 a.m. Friday morning. I've just got time to write to you before my next parade which is at 11.30 a.m. I shouldn't have time to write tonight because I'm on defaulters' parade, staff parade, Last Post parade and orderly corporals' parade.

I've been terribly busy this morning. There's a big ceremonial parade coming off in Milan in the near future. It's probably a farewell march-past for some big shot who is perhaps getting demobbed. I've been on quite a number of these parades before, so it's my job now to drill these blokes for it. I've been shouting all morning and my throat is sore.

I went into Milan last night, and to my surprise all the Italian bars, shops and cinemas were closed. The reason was that there had been a strike. The trams were running, and I saw an Italian jump on the tram as it was moving. He jumped on the driver and threw him out into the street and a real riot started then, but I don't know what it was all about. The biggest percentage of the women in Milan are nothing but prostitutes.

I went to the pictures last night and saw Ralph Bellamy in *Guest in the House*, not bad but a rather slow beginning.

Before I go any further, I must thank you for your two letters dated 22nd and 25th December which I received today. You've made a good start for the bottom drawer! Thank you for the cutting, it was nice of you to put it in the *Observer*.[10] Like you, I

10 The local newspaper in Rochdale.

want everyone to know. I hope you went to London with Mash. I'm sure she looked forward to it especially after you've both planned it for such a long time.[11] Don't be afraid to do anything without asking me because I leave it to you. I shall never tell you what to do. Don't worry what you've spent on Christmas presents, it only comes once a year. You made my mouth water when I read what you'd had for Christmas dinner!

7.1.46.

The Italians are still on strike. The reasons are firstly hunger, and secondly because when the war finished the partisans were given extra pay and the rest of the soldiers were promised more money later and they haven't had it so far. It's not safe walking about on your own in Milan because you're liable to get a knife in the back.

10.1.46.

It's 10.20 Thursday night. I'm writing this in the guard room, it's terribly cold and wet outside, so it's thanks to my stripe I'm not standing outside doing the guard. The shops, etc. are still closed in Milan but the Italians appear to have quietened down a bit.

I took the guards' dinner into Milan today. They're guarding a vehicle car park which is quite close to where I had my photo taken. I called to see if the copies were ready but the answer was,

---

11   Hilda's diary shows that apart from having several meals in restaurants, she and her friend saw Tommy Trinder at the London Palladium, went to an exhibition of Picasso and Matisse at the Victoria & Albert Museum, saw *Brief Encounter*, went to an exhibition of Paul Klee at the Tate Gallery, went shopping in Selfridges and Harrods, and saw *The Rake's Progress*, amongst other things…

"Come back tomorrow". That's quite a regular saying with the Italians.

You asked me how I spent the New Year. Well, it just seemed like an ordinary day to me. I was in bed and asleep before the New Year came in, but before I went to sleep, I said a little prayer for us both.

Yes, if we have our honeymoon in winter we'll go to London. I've seen quite a lot of the place. I've never liked it since I've been in the army because it's been one mad rush on buses, Tubes, trains through crowds of people. Travelling in the army is no enjoyment.

I can't help but smile at some of the lads when they sit down to write a letter. They say, "I'll be damned if I know what to write about". They always say to me, "I don't know what you find to write about, Ronnie"; even though I have no news I have everything to write about to you.

I'm always thinking about you. I think – it's 7.15 a.m. and Hilda will be getting up, about 9 a.m. I think of you at school, 12 to 1.30 you're having dinner[12], 4.20 you'll probably be getting on the bus for home, 5.10 p.m. you're home. On Monday night you're at night school and sometimes on Wednesday nights you go with your mother to the Carlton[13] for tea. Friday nights you go to Bill's and on Saturday or Sunday you can stay in bed a little longer: you're never out of my thoughts.

13.1.46.

I've just been told I've got to take some prisoners to a town called Brescia about sixty miles from here, so here's hoping my map-reading won't fail me. I'll be back tomorrow so I'll write

---

12   When Ronnie talks about "dinner" and "tea" he is using the Lancashire terms for midday and evening meals respectively.

13   A large restaurant and dance hall in the centre of Rochdale.

to you then. I didn't want you to wait for these photos, so I'm
enclosing them with this letter.

I must close now: all the blokes who are going with me are
ready and I haven't packed my kit yet.

15.1.46.

I've just arrived back from Brescia, the place where I took the
prisoners. They were British soldiers who had committed crimes.
One bloke's crime went as far back as January '45 for being two
days absent in the line. He got three years' penal servitude for that.
Another bloke got two years for escaping from a prison camp. If
you do a crime in the army you certainly pay for it in a big way.
Touch wood I've got a clean sheet and it's staying that way.[14] The
trouble is, some of these young lads are easily led astray by the older
men. That's one thing about me, in the army I've thought and done
things for myself. It's surprising how you can tell what a person is
like. For instance three of the blokes who were in the convoy with
me yesterday were typical rogues. They asked me if they could go for
a walk. I thought there was something funny and I knew it wasn't
for the good of their health. You see these last few days there's been
an awful lot of kit, etc. stolen out of the billets and I'd a good idea
who was stealing it. However, I let these blokes go for a walk and I
followed them, and not to my surprise I saw them selling an Italian
some army kit. I went straight up to them and put the three of them
on a charge. Since I arrived back, they've been charged and they all
got fifty-six days' detention and believe me they deserve it. I don't
care how much of their own kit they sell, but to steal off their mates
is the worst crime ever. It was lucky I didn't have anything stolen,
however I was right in guessing who the thieves were.

---

14 Ronnie's only transgression, ever, in the army, is that in the following
months he would take slightly more leave than he was due, because he
was so desperate to be with Hilda.

While in Brescia yesterday I called in an Italian school just to look round. There was only the caretaker there so he showed me the place. The classrooms are arranged just like ours. I stood in one of the classrooms and looked about me. Everything was quiet and a hard lump came in my throat. I seemed to see children and there was you talking to them. I can't tell you how I felt. Believe me I had to walk out of that school in a hurry or I think I'd have started to cry.

I'm not quite certain yet how much I'll get for a gratuity, but I think it will be in the region of £100. Of course if I get another stripe it means more money and I realise how much we'll need. At present, including this stripe, I get seven shillings a day, a big difference from when I came in the army when I was getting two shillings and nine pence a day.[15] Out of the seven shillings, I allow Mother two shillings a day, so I draw five shillings. I haven't decided what I'm going to do when I get demobbed but I don't think I'll go back to Robinson's. Prospects were very poor; you had to wait for someone to die before you got a decent job.[16]

This time last year I was in the line up in the mountains near Bologna, going out on fighting patrols into German lines. Every shell or mortar I thought was meant for me, it just had to be that I lived to see the day when I met you.

18.1.46.

I'm writing this in a lorry going to Bologna. I'd only been back a day from the last convoy to Brescia when I had to get ready to go on this one. We're thirty-one miles from Bologna and this convoy is going at ten miles an hour. The roads are about three feet thick with snow, it's freezing and I don't know how I'm managing to hold this pen but if I don't write now it means waiting another two

---

15 13.75 pence a day in decimal currency.
16 Yet, despite his misgivings, Ronnie did go back there...

or three days. Last night we slept in a vehicle park, and about 3 a.m. this morning we were awakened by the sound of rifles firing. They were firing at Italians who took the wheels off some of the vehicles. We had to get up then and start chasing them and did I do some cursing. Two Italians were shot and we found three tyres. There are still three wheels missing so one truck had to stay behind. I suppose there will be a stink about that when we get back. I don't like these convoys in this cold weather: they never give you time to do your own little jobs; I'll have hundreds of them to do when I get back. I've been to Bologna before. We entered it with the Indians the same day as it fell. I suppose it was a nice place once but it suffered very heavily from the war. This convoy contains medical supplies for a hospital in Bologna. We'll have to watch it at the next stop, or should I say watch the Italians.

Cpl. R.H.Williams[17]

"C" Coy 2nd Loyals

C.M.F.

21.1.46.

It's 2 a.m. Monday and I've just arrived back from the convoy. I feel dead tired as I haven't slept for three nights so this letter will be short. I couldn't have gone to bed without writing to you, however. It's been a long tiring journey. Milan is feet deep in snow but it's a little warmer now.

Well, darling, it's now full corporal. That's not bad going, is it? They couldn't have given it me any quicker, you've got to hold one stripe for twenty-one days before you get paid for it. I'd only held it twenty days and now I've got my second one.

---

17   Ronnie gets his second promotion within an extraordinarily short space of time.

23.1.46.

Yesterday I was acting orderly sergeant, and a very busy day it was. I was out of bed at 6 a.m., and took staff parade at 6.10 a.m., woke the boys up 6.15, and took staff parade 6.30, saw to it that everybody had had breakfast by 7 a.m., and then up to 8 a.m. was my own time to wash, shave and have my breakfast. 8.05 a.m. I was taking the men on drill parade which lasted until 9 a.m. I could hardly speak when I came off that. 9.15 orderly sergeant's report to RSM for tomorrow's detail. 10 a.m. I had a drink of tea, or that's what the so-called cook called it; I haven't had a good drink since I've been in the Loyals. 11 a.m. I went for the mail; there were only about twenty letters but I had three of them, two from you and one from my mother. 12 noon I got the defaulters on parade and inspected them, 12.15 I wrote the strength of the boys for rations, etc., 12.30 I went round with the orderly officer to ask if there were any complaints, and there were! 1.15 p.m. I had my dinner, 2 p.m. staff parade, 2.30 COS orders, 3 p.m. I saw the men off on night guards, up to 4 p.m. I was writing orders and sick reports for the following day; at 4 p.m. I mounted the battalion guard, 4.30 teatime, 5 p.m. defaulters again, 6 o'clock I was on telephone duties, 7 p.m. I was on duty in the canteen or corporals' mess until 10 p.m., 10.15 staff parade, 10.30 p.m. I went round to see all the lights were out, 10.45 I was in bed.

It's now 7 p.m. Wednesday, and I'm writing this in the guard room 59 Area Headquarters Milan. The weather is terrible. It's done nothing but snow for a fortnight now.

Your letters I received are dated 12th and 14th January.[18] What a shock I got when I knew Mac was killed. You have my deepest sympathy. I know what he meant to you when you knew him from being a pup and saw him grow up. You looked upon him as something more than a dog, as you say you thought of him as a friend. I can't tell you how sorry I am, but if you haven't another dog when I get home, I'll get you one. Don't cry, it makes me sad when I know you cry.

Yes, I suppose it will be hard settling down to civilian life after four years in the army. In the army everything is so regular, routine, etc. I'll miss my friends, and comradeship is a big thing in the army. You pull together through thick and thin and share each other's joys and sorrows. I noticed when I was home last, some people had already forgotten there had been a war on and that men had fought, given their lives so others might live. When I get back to civvy street I know from what I've seen that I'll have to look after myself.

26.1.46.

I received a letter from Bill yesterday, he said you'd been so busy lately he'd only seen you once since Christmas. Annie[19] asked me if I'm ready for the wedding which you talk about so much.

You asked me when I expect to be demobbed. As I said before I don't know but my guess is about October.

---

18 According to Hilda's diary entry of 14th January her young dog Mac spotted her on the other side of the main road and rushed across to her although she told him to stay. He was killed instantly by a car, which was dreadfully unlucky at a time when there was little passing traffic, even on the main route from Lancashire to Yorkshire. Hilda grieved for him and told the story for many years afterwards.

19 Bill's wife.

Good luck with your play[20], I shall be thinking about you. I wish I could have been there.

I'm sure it was hard work at the dancing class but it's a change for you. So, people tell you you are getting slimmer!

I've not been too busy today, mostly drill parades. I've been shouting my head off lately. They are certainly tightening up on discipline; fourteen men on charges this morning for failing to comply with battalion orders, i.e. not having a spare pair of laces on kit inspection. They all got fourteen days' detention; a bit heavy, what!

It's 11.30 p.m. and I'm writing this sitting on my bed. It's very cold in this room, no fires or heating except for this candle which I can just about see to write this letter with.

29.1.46.

I've done nothing but lecture today. Firstly it was the Bren gun and then mortars, grenades, rifles, and Tommy guns. It was for the benefit of the new recruits we've got. The chaps who came out of the artillery with me and the other old soldiers were really browned off. I couldn't blame them feeling that way because they know the weapons inside out. I like taking lectures, time passes much more quickly and you don't get bored.

Yesterday I was on guard at the vehicle park, Milan. It was a very busy day for me. You've got to back lorries in and out; over 400 came in so you can tell how busy I was.

Had a letter from Mother today. She said she's going to your house for tea and then to your play. I hope she likes it and that you were a success. I'd love to see you in your new dress, I'm sure you look beautiful in it.

---

20 Hilda was a member of a local amateur dramatics group which was putting on a play, as well as going regularly to dancing classes and evening classes.

1.2.46.

Once again, I'm going with a convoy. It's only a short journey this time, fifty-five miles to a town called Ferrara. I'm taking some British soldiers to a prison there who are going to do imprisonment of two years and over.

I've been terribly busy. We're very much below strength owing to men being demobbed so it means we've got to do two jobs. I should be in charge of about twenty men, instead I've got forty. I've been reading in the paper about fog in Blighty. It must have arrived here because this last week there's been nothing but fog. It's just the thing for these black-market blokes; they can go about their work unseen.

This battalion is moving to Austria any time between 14th and 22nd February to a place called Wildon near the city of Graz and north-east of Klagenfurt. We are taking over from the 16th battalion Durham Light Infantry which is being disbanded owing to most of their men being demobbed. This affects quite a number of units in Italy. I think we'll be doing guards there, I'm not certain yet, but the reason there are troops in Austria is in case Tito starts trouble. We did that sort of job before on the Yugoslav border and in the mountains so I hope it's not the same again. It's about 250 miles to Austria from Milan; there will be two or three days travelling.

[Included with this letter is part of a poem, which Hilda must have started to write to Ronnie after she received the letter:

"How shall I write you words,
Coin phrases which tell
You of my love? I know not.
Yet, as I write, the greyness
Of this February day, the still

Monotony of quiet air and limpid
Sky, are quickened by a throbbing
Memory, that as I pause, dances
Before my thinking eyes, and
Glides into my words as I now write,
And fills me with the kindness of our
Love and the keenness of our parting."]

4.2.46.

I'm writing this sitting in the wagon, we've just left Rimini. I told you in my last letter I was going with a convoy to Ferrara with some prisoners. However when we arrived there the prison was full, that was 2 a.m., and we had to go another ninety-five miles to Rimini. I could hardly keep my eyes open. The reason for taking so long was a terrible fog. We are just passing through the town of Piacenza. The kids are running about in their bare feet. They certainly must be tough.

7.2.46.

We should have arrived back from Rimini two days ago, but owing to bad luck our truck broke down. That's the second time with two convoys and they always break down miles from anywhere. This time the front axle snapped so we had to wait five hours before a wagon came along to pick us up or tow us back. Some of the roads are terribly steep and winding and with continually keeping the brakes on they set on fire. The canvas roof was burnt out and some of our kits, but luckily not mine. However, we got things under control and were once again on our way.

This morning I received your very beautiful birthday present. You couldn't have sent anything better, it's just what I wanted.

I've been keeping my letters and writing paper in between bits of cardboard. I can't thank you enough.[21]

10.2.46.

Will I be your Valentine? I certainly will! Thank you for the birthday card, the words couldn't have been better.

I've kept all your letters and what a pile there is. I'll need a kit bag for them soon! During my quiet moments, which are very few, I read your letters time and time again and your photos are getting endless kisses.

I went into Milan last night by myself because everybody else was on guard. It's terrible going out alone but I did see some blokes who used to be in my platoon. I'd seen all the films before, so I went to La Scala to see *Carmen*[22], it was brilliant.

I want to get married as soon as I get settled in civvy street and that won't take me long. I want to get a decent job or wage.

By the way, we move to Austria on 20th February so think of me from the 20th to about the 23rd on my way.

11.2.46.

Enclosed are two pairs of stockings. Are they fully fashioned?[23] They are terribly dear but they're the best I've seen so far. I hope you like them.

---

21 The present for Ronnie's birthday on 16th February was a writing case. It is there with all their other mementos of the time.

22 One cannot help but smile at the fact that the cinema was full, so Ronnie went to La Scala instead! He always did like opera, for the rest of his life.

23 Predictably and endearingly, Ronnie had absolutely no knowledge of anything to do with things like stockings.

I'm playing football this afternoon against the 6th Armoured Brigade at the Milan stadium.

13.2.46.

This is going to be very short: I've just been told I've to hand over all stores and equipment to an artillery unit which is taking over some of our guards before we go to Austria. By the time I finish that job it will be at least 11 o'clock tonight: I'll write a long letter to you tomorrow.

14.2.46.

I went to the pictures a few nights ago; George Formby in *He Snoops to Conquer*, not very good. I laughed during the showing of the news. It showed police (civilian and military) carrying out a check-up on the black market in Europe. The speaker said, "The amazing part about it was, not one soldier was found indulging in it". You should have heard the roar that went up; soldiers are the biggest offenders on the black market.

20.2.46.

It's 7.30 a.m. Wednesday morning and we move off at 8.15 a.m. to Austria. Everybody is rushing around like fools. I haven't even packed my kit yet and I'm in charge of the baggage at 8 a.m. We march to the station with all the kit, arrive there about 11 a.m., but the train doesn't set off until 9 o'clock tonight. Just think, we've got to hang about the station all day. I believe we arrive at our destination in Austria 10.30 p.m. Friday. The worst part about it is we've got to march nineteen miles when we get off the train and with full equipment too.

23.2.46.

We've just arrived at Wildon in Austria. It was a long, tiring journey. What a march it was from our billets in Milan to the central station. It was only five miles but the sun was boiling hot and did I sweat. The first stop was Udine then we started to go north. Our next stop was Trieste and then through the outskirts of Venice. Up to there the scenery was nothing but fields and rivers. Then we were in Austria, and our next stop was Villach. Each of the stops we had a meal. You can tell the difference as soon as you get into Austria: everything is much cleaner than it is in Italy. The houses are much like the English type. All the way into Austria were mountains, lakes and waterfalls. It was a lovely sight at night when the sun was setting on top of the mountains and the moon shining on the lakes. The last stop was the city of Graz, which has been badly damaged with bombs and shellfire. It's much colder in Austria, which was a big help for the nineteen-mile route march. Wildon is twelve miles from Graz where our battalion headquarters are, but C Company is another seven miles further on. The march wasn't too bad but I feel just about all in now. There were eight of us in the carriage, we were just packed like sardines and we had all our kit too. We were three nights on the train and I don't think I slept three hours all the time, there wasn't enough room to sleep. Most of the time I was reading. I had a pile of papers and books from Mother just before I left Milan, *Rochdale Observer*, *News of the World*, etc., so they kept me busy.

Now, about this place. Well, we're right out in the wilds, billeted in a castle, a weird old place. The nearest thing to us is a farm half a mile away and the nearest town is Graz nineteen miles away. I'm certainly going to miss going to the canteen and pictures once in a while. Surrounding the castle are mountains and trees. I believe we are here to do training, field craft, weapons, grenades, etc. There are three battalions in this area; two are training while the other is patrolling the Austrian border. There have been one or two small riots on the border so we're here to keep order. That's about all I know at the moment. There's nothing nice about this place, everything seems dead, but being in a place like this I should be able to save my money.

Of course all the Austrians speak German so I'll have to learn another language, that is if I see any Austrians to speak to. So far, it's not like the Austria you think of with music, etc., this place is just one wilderness. It will be nicer in summer when we can go swimming or sunbathing.

It's dinnertime so I'll close now but I will write again soon. After dinner I'm taking the lads out to chop some trees down for our fires.

26.2.46.

I haven't had a letter from you since I came here, but that can be expected since we're miles from anywhere. I suppose I'll get a pile all at once.

I've just about settled down here. Everything is in such a mix-up, it's always the same when the battalion moves.

I've been working night and day. There's all the admin to be done. I'm also in charge of PT. Since 8 o'clock this morning I've been working in the gym, making improvised equipment: horsebox, horizontal bars, boxing ring, etc. Of course I'm nowhere near finished, it will take at least another week. The open-air PT has certainly made me feel fit but I felt terribly hungry. We don't get enough food.

I had to take some blokes to the dentist yesterday to a town called Leibnitz. What a job I had trying to find the place without being able to speak the language. All the lads were roaring with laughter but they changed their tune when they entered the dentist's.

These Austrians look just like the Germans, blonde hair, blue eyes and high cheekbones. This part of Austria seems to be worse off for food and clothing than any part of Italy.

It's terribly cold here. My hands have been chapped rather badly so I've had to put some ointment on. It snowed a bit yesterday.

They've certainly tightened up on discipline. Any man caught doing anything wrong or late on parade is put on a charge which means twenty-eight days' detention or more. NCOs have to be called by their rank and not their first name.

I'll be very busy tomorrow: 8 o'clock PT, 9 o'clock rifle drill, 10 o'clock map reading, 11 o'clock instruction on Vickers guns, 2 o'clock sport, 3 o'clock admin, but I don't mind being busy. The days pass by and every day is one nearer to the day when we shall be together again.

1.3.46.

This morning myself and six men went out on a security patrol, checking the identity of all civilians because there are supposed to be some suspicious people knocking about. We checked a few, who proved their identity. I had to make a report out stating whether the civilians were friendly or otherwise. We set off at 8 o'clock this morning and didn't get back until 3 o'clock this afternoon, walking all the time. We were without food all that time.

4.3.46.

Everybody in the battalion has to learn to ski. We go out in the mountains about sixteen miles from here. I shan't be back until

10 o'clock tonight. It's all infantry training using skis. It's terribly hard work but it won't be too bad after a week or two of training. What a sensation it is going down the mountains. The average mountain is 1,300 feet high. The snow has been coming down very heavily today so it makes it easier to ski. I thought I'd had it yesterday racing down the mountain; I just missed a tree and my heart was in my mouth. The hardest part of skiing is turning which is very awkward. They issue special boots, a peaked cap, leather suit, eye shields and leather gloves. It's going to be a mix-up skiing in the dark tonight but I'll be careful what I'm doing.

I didn't come back from the skiing until teatime last night, and after tea I went out on a security patrol. What a terrible night it was; snow, rain and mud. Some of these Austrian maps are terrible to read. First-class roads are marked as second class and they go as far as putting them as bridle paths. It's a good job I had an idea where I was going.

Tomorrow I'm on carriers. I've only been on them three times and I'm instructing on them tomorrow. It didn't take me long to pick it up. I'm not quite conversant with the gear changing, but practice will remedy that. Tomorrow I'm also taking squad drill, PT and boxing, so I should be fit after all this week.

There's nothing here at all, but it's surprising how you can fill your time at night. During the day it's all training, so your own jobs have to wait until night, scrubbing equipment, polishing brasses, sewing, darning, washing clothes, writing letters. We have a kit inspection every morning, and for eight mornings on a run my room (six men) has been the cleanest and smartest. Of course the credit goes to the NCO, but it's the way you treat the men; there is a right way and a wrong way. The officer in this company is a typical bully and wants the NCOs to be the same. I think that's a poor way. I get a lot more out of the men than the NCO who bullies them.

7.3.46.

I haven't been skiing today. I've been on one of those security patrols again. We went about sixty miles in a Bren carrier in pouring rain, so I decided to take shelter. I went to a farmhouse, where they fried me two eggs, and gave me bread and wine. I was glad of it. Three blokes with me got the same. We could only speak a few words but we gave them cigarettes which they jumped at.

All officers and NCOs in this battalion were given a lecture by the divisional commander yesterday. He said we're here because trouble is expected from Tito. This is now a regular battalion, and as long as troops are needed in Austria this battalion will stay here so it looks as though I'll spend the rest of my time abroad in Austria which isn't a very bright outlook. He went on to say each battalion in the division would take it in turns to go to Vienna and do a month's guards there. The Russians control Vienna, but there are also units of the United Nations' troops there. The Loyals should go in about two months' time. During the early part of summer each battalion does a month's infantry training under canvas, PT courses, etc. He also said there may be an odd vacancy for NCOs to go to Blighty on courses, so if there's any chance of a course in this battalion, this is one NCO who will be there. He asked if there are any questions so I asked him about leave to Blighty. As far as he knew we only get twenty-eight days a year. I had to wait over two and a half years for my last one, so the new idea is an improvement but it's still not good enough. I said to him "Why not have fourteen days every six months?". His reply was "Transport won't permit". Anyway, if I'm not demobbed, I should get a leave next October so it's something to look forward to.

I told you I was getting 6s. 6d a day for my first stripe. I got paid for my second a few weeks ago and I'm now getting 7s. 4d a day.[24] There's nothing to spend your money on here except in the canteen so I'm saving up very well now.

Tomorrow all day I'm giving lectures on weapons and infantry tactics so there will be plenty of talking to do.

9.3.46.

Enclosed are two pairs of fully fashioned stockings. They are the ones I got in Milan. I suppose by this time you've received the others. I do hope you like them. I send them with all my love and only wish I could get more.

10.3.46.

What, another play! You are going to be busy; I wish I could be in it with you. You should be 100 per cent fit after all this dancing, PT and swimming. Wouldn't it be nice if I could be there to do all those things with you?

Talk about being fit, I certainly feel it what with this skiing and PT, and yesterday I played football. What a game it was; pools of water on the pitch, mud and pouring with rain. We played the tank corps and won by seven goals to five. What a score! I was covered in mud all over. The blokes laughed when I skidded in front of the goal and went flying in the back of the net. It took three blokes to sort me out of the net.

I had a letter from a bloke at Robinson's, the one I wrote to telling him I was engaged. He told all the girls about it and most of them saw the announcement in the *Observer*. He said, "You should have seen Betty Grindrod's face, it changed colour". Poor Betty, she tried like all the girls to get me but they all failed.

I just left off a few minutes there because I just received your

---

24 About 37p in today's currency.

parcel. It's terribly sweet of you, I can't thank you enough. You don't know how glad I am of the toothpaste, we can't get any at all here. I wrote to Mother last week telling her I was on my last tube. It's lovely of you to send the chocolate.

12.3.46.

I've just arrived back from a patrol. I went out alone tonight on a motorbike. It was terribly cold, but much better than walking ninety miles – that was the distance I went. Everything was quiet and peaceful. I took a short cut through the woods, and was amazed to see about sixty deer running through the trees. It was a lovely sight with the moon shining on the trees and the sound of a waterfall in the distance. I stopped the bike engine running and sat there listening and thinking of you.

I'm not surprised you are sick and tired of restrictions, rationing, state control, etc. Though I haven't lived in Blighty for three years I've had a good idea how bad things really are, especially on my last leave. I suppose it will be the same for a number of years yet.

You're like me then, you're not sure which political party you support. It's a Labour Government, but like any other party there's never the right person in the right job.

The day I left you to come back to Italy my heart was aching with happiness. It was the sort of feeling you only get once in a lifetime, we were meant for each other. When I start talking about you, I could go on forever. Some day I'll write a book about you and you'll be surprised how much I could write about one person.

15.3.46.

Thank you from the bottom of my heart for the parcel containing the cake and books. The cake is beautiful, please thank your mother. Someday I'll be able to do something in return for her kindness. I'm really glad of the books.

You certainly like sunshine, don't you? I do, but I've seen the time when I've hated it. That was in the desert with nothing but toil and sweat. I was almost black in those days, wearing only a pair of shorts until sunset. But they will be different conditions when I'm with you and I won't hate the sun.

Here are a few answers to your queries. I came abroad on 14th June 1943, and arrived in Gibraltar where we stayed for three months. I was in the Royal Artillery then, mostly spit and polish and working in the tunnels, but with lots of sport. Left Gibraltar in September and arrived in Bone, North Africa. From there we moved all over Africa dragging our guns along. We went on to Algiers, Oran, Tunis, Tripoli, in December landed in Sicily, Messina, Palermo, Catania (near Mount Etna), Syracuse. In February 1944 we moved on to Anzio, and there we had two months of hell, next Cassino, two months of bringing Jerry planes down as fast as they came over, but sometimes we got the biggest smack. I think the Yanks bombed our own troops more than the Jerries did. July, we stayed in Naples for three weeks then had a mad rush through Rome, then the Gothic line where we withdrew for three weeks' rest, but during that time we trained all day so we wouldn't get idle. On to Florence, Leghorn, Ancona and dozens of small towns. October, we came back to Naples, where we and practically all units of the artillery broke up and were transferred into the infantry, the worst thing that could have happened. The reason for the disbanding of the artillery was because the Jerries had very few planes left, and it was all infantry, and boy, did we get the dirty work to do. October to December we did infantry training just outside Naples. During that time I went on a six-week PT and tough tactics course: assault course, boxing, wrestling, unarmed combat, etc. January, we set off to join the Lancashire Fusiliers in the line but the Loyals who had just come overseas needed reinforcements and we joined them. We did another two months' training with them and in March went on the line again. The line was then static as it had been for the last few months. We were on Monte Grande, and on a clear day you could see Bologna. That was a cruel two months lying in slit trenches and climbing mountains great enough to break your heart. April came and the big push started. We went through Bologna, Ferrara and Venice (supposed to be the most beautiful city in the world today). There Jerry packed it in, and what a great day that was. I shall never forget it as long as I live. I thank God I've been spared through all that hell and misery. Since then we've travelled quite a bit. Trieste, Genoa, Milan and now Austria. I've seen quite a bit of the world in a rough sort of way but I've a lot to be thankful for, and I am.

18.3.46.

I've just been told I've got to go on patrol so I'll write as much as I can in the short time available.

It will be 12 o'clock tonight before I get back. Myself and twelve men are going to the Yugoslav border and checking the identity of all persons and vehicles. There are supposed to have been nine lorries stolen and the Yugoslavs are suspected. I won't go too near the border because they are very quick on the trigger if they see anyone trying to cross the border. I've just looked at the map and there's nothing but mountains where we're going. I'm going so far in the carrier, and will have to walk the rest of the way.

Two days ago I was chopping great trees down in the forest, and boy, are my arms stiff now. All this training will either make me or break me.

Tomorrow I'm skiing until noon. During the afternoon there's PT, boxing and carrier maintenance. At night I'm on patrol again so I won't have any time to do my own work. During the night all units in Austria send out patrols. We're falling over each other in the dark. I laughed the other night at an NCO from the King's Liverpool Regiment. He came up to me and asked me where he was and I told him. He said, "Blimey, I must've had the map upside down", and his compass was on the wrong bearing.

What do you think of the Churchill-Stalin argument? Stalin says Churchill is a warmonger. We knew that without being told.

I often think of the first time I kissed you, remember? I'd only known you a day, but it seemed like a lifetime. I'd seen you that Friday at Bill's and the next time I called he asked me if I'd like a date with you. Though I'd never been out with a girl before something told me not to miss this opportunity and believe me, I asked Bill every night if he'd arrange that date. I enjoyed that night more than I'd enjoyed any night during my life. Even though I'm far away today, I'm just as happy because I know I'll be coming back to that same true love and happiness.

21.3.46.

Thank you for your letter dated 10th March. Yes, I read about the disaster at Bolton in the paper. It must have been shocking. I realise how you felt when you wondered if your father was in that disaster.[25] No wonder you prayed. Yes, a thing like that makes you realise how much you think of people. A similar

---

25 On 9th March at a football match between Bolton Wanderers and Stoke City at the Bolton ground, barriers collapsed as a result of overcrowding. Thirty-three people were killed and approximately 400 were injured. As this letter indicates, Wilfred, Hilda's father, was at the match. The family heard about the tragedy on the radio, and had no idea until he eventually got back home whether he was safe or not. They had no telephone until the 1950s, and were understandably frantic.

incident happened at the Rochdale rugby ground in 1938 when the stand collapsed and hundreds were injured, but people who cause these happenings are not fit to be called human beings. I don't blame you for never liking football again.

I'm certainly glad your father got home safely, you had me worried when I was reading the letter.

Well, this is terrific news: you remember the NCOs courses to Blighty I told you about? I'm going on a leadership course to Warminster. It starts about 10th April and I think it will last a few weeks. When it's finished I'll get leave home. By the time I write again I should know more details. I'm really excited about it, and I know you will be. Aren't I lucky to be the first to go? There are very few courses going to Blighty. I told you I wouldn't let you down if I got the chance to come home. When I get to London, I can ring you up.

You asked me when I have leave. I should say about May, as the course should be over by then, perhaps before.

24.3.46.

It's 10.55 p.m. Sunday and I'm writing this in the corporals' mess. Ten minutes ago I arrived back from skiing and I'm dead tired now. We climbed 1,500 feet and raced down it in two and a half minutes. At that rate we were going thirty-five miles an hour, you feel as though you have wings. I laughed at one bloke; he'd gone about halfway down the mountain when he fell and all you could see was a little ball rolling down the mountain. Skiing finishes at the end of March because the snow is gradually melting away.

There are now four horses in this company and anyone can ride them. We have an Austrian instructor: he took me the other night. It's very nice at night when you've nothing to do.

It was such a beautiful day yesterday – I went swimming for an hour in a lake just on the borders of Austria and Yugoslavia.

I did enjoy it, it was as calm as a pond. How I wished you could have been with me.

I haven't heard anything more about the course yet but I suppose they will let me know at the last minute. All I know is it is supposed to start on 8ᵗʰ April. To get there for the 8ᵗʰ I'll have to go sometime this week. I'm certainly looking forward to it.

26.3.46.

I'm in a terrific hurry, I've just got twenty minutes to write this and pack my kit and be at Graz station by 11.30 p.m. Yes, I'm bound for dear old Blighty! I'll write to you as soon as I get there. It will take about five days from Villach.

Cpl. R.H. Williams
"C" Coy
School of Infantry
Warminster
Wilts.

5.4.46.

It's 10 p.m., and I arrived at Warminster at 7 p.m. I caught the 9.20 a.m. from Manchester, the only stops were at Crewe and then Bristol, arriving at Bristol at 4 p.m., so it took about seven hours and it's another two hours from Bristol to Warminster.

I asked if we get weekends off and we get three during the course, from 9 o'clock Saturday morning to 23.59 hours Sunday night. As you can see it's a hopeless job trying to get home for a weekend. It would cost a lot but I'm not worried about that, it's just the travelling time is too much. I heard we may get three or four days at Easter. If I do, I'll come home then without fail.

Well, there's nothing at Warminster except a few houses and one cinema, all you can see is NCOs and more NCOs and barracks.

I believe it's a long, tough course but I'll stick it.

Gosh, I miss you, those few days I've just spent at home with you were heaven on earth. I do feel lonely tonight but I know you are thinking about me.[26]

8.4.46.

This has been my first night off since I came here. We started training last Saturday morning, and have been at it ever since. Saturday and Sunday nights we were out training until 11 p.m. They don't intend wasting time, do they?

Ninety per cent of the blokes here are acting unpaid lance corporals and have been in the army a few weeks, and boy, are they mad on the army. In the barrack room at night they're throwing rifles about, marching up and down or reading pamphlets. They even talk about it in their sleep.

It's just like joining the army again, but I realise it's better doing it here than in Austria.

It's pretty certain I'll get three or four days home at Easter; a few days together is better than nothing, isn't it?

Could I ring you up anywhere? Could you give me a number and let me know what time to ring you?[27]

10.4.46.

I've been terribly busy, they keep you on your feet all day. My throat is sore with shouting and lecturing; three hours on the barrack square this morning. I finished at 7 o'clock tonight, every other night has been 8 o'clock, and then I've written pages

---

26 Ronnie had clearly been allowed a brief visit home before starting his course.
27 Their calls had to be arranged in advance, from one public telephone box to another.

and pages of notes on the course. There's a canteen and a cinema but I haven't had time to go to them. The food is good and plenty of it.

14.4.46.

I've just been on the telephone to you, it was wonderful to hear your voice but I didn't like the way we were cut off. I tried to get through again but the exchange wouldn't allow it. They said we'd had seven minutes five seconds. Never mind, I'll ring you again on Thursday in Blackpool.[28]

I've decided you'd better not book for me at Blackpool because I may not have enough money. The fare to Manchester is 39s. 11d then it will be extra to Rochdale. I'm mad at not being able to draw out of our credits and there's no way of getting extra money.

Tomorrow will be a busy day for me. My first subject is weapons, drilling, PT, field craft, aircraft recognition, and then I've got to talk for two hours on map reading.

18.4.46.

(Written to Hilda already in Blackpool)

It's wonderful to speak to you on the phone. I can't thank you enough for the ticket to Blackpool. As I told you over the phone, I managed to borrow £5 from one of the sergeants here,

---

28 It turned out that by bad luck Hilda would be on a course in Blackpool when Ronnie was due to have his leave, and he was clearly struggling to find enough money to join her.

I'll pay him back later on.[29] It's terrible to be without money but we'll manage all right. I'm really glad there's room for me where you're staying. If I'd gone to a YMCA, I'd probably have been miles away from you.

23.4.46.

(Hilda is still in Blackpool)

I can't tell you how I feel. I'm so sad and yet so happy. What a day that will be when I come home and never need to say goodbye again. Blackpool was so crowded but I enjoyed every moment of it with you. I'm too full for words, I think you know that, every time I leave you. Will write tomorrow night and ring you Thursday.

24.4.46.

On the way back there should have been a special train but the railway as usual made a mess of it. I dashed across the Underground to Paddington where I got the 9.25 to Swindon arriving there 11.40, changed for Warminster but the train didn't stop there. The nearest station was Westby, arrived there 1.30 a.m. so I had nine miles to walk to Warminster where I met some of the boys. Up to that time I'd come all the way alone, it was terribly dark and 4 o'clock this morning when I arrived in camp. I had two hours' sleep.

---

29 To give an indication of the value of £5 at the time, in her diary for 1945-46 Hilda had obviously been working out how much she could afford to save towards the wedding. After tax and superannuation had been deducted her average weekly net salary was £4 6s. 1d. However, the letters, mostly Hilda's only way of communicating with Ronnie, were not a major expenditure. According to the printed information in her 1947 diary, letters and postcards to HM Forces abroad cost 1 ½d for the first ounce of weight, then 1d for each additional ounce.

It was awful travelling, with thousands of people; I had to stand for most of the journey. I had a cup of tea and a sandwich and that's all until breakfast this morning. I've been thinking of you all day on your course. It was wonderful with you in Blackpool, how I wish I could be there now. But don't worry, I'll be seeing you in just over three weeks' time. This will be my last letter to you in Blackpool. I'll send the next to Rochdale.

29.4.46.

I am looking forward to seeing you on Saturday; it's wonderful. This time last week we were together in Blackpool but it seems like years. It's terribly sweet of you to come to London and see me. Let me know what time you arrive at Euston and I'll be waiting for you. I'll be thinking of you at school tomorrow, remember me to all at home.

1.5.46.

This half of the course is certainly tough but boy, is it worth it to see you. You should have seen the state I came back in the other morning, wet through, covered in mud and my face black with paint, four hours in bed and start work again.

Well, I've got my railway warrant for Saturday in London, 17s. 11d, so it's not too bad. I'll be waiting for you at Euston, this will be my last letter until I see you.

2.5.46.

I wrote to you last night and said it would be my last letter until I saw you on Saturday. I don't suppose this will arrive until

Saturday morning and you'll be on your way to London by then but it will be waiting for you when you get back.

I just had to write again to thank you for your terrific letter dated 30th April. After this weekend all I will be thinking of is my next leave with you which will be in a fortnight's time. I haven't forgotten your play on 18th May. I should be coming home that day.

7.5.46.

It's all bed and work here and I'm only just getting over that glorious weekend. I arrived back Sunday 11.30 p.m. and lay thinking about you for hours. All the blokes asked me what sort of weekend I'd had. I told them it was terrific and you paid for everything. It was awful on the scheme last night; bitter cold, my feet were wet after walking in streams and rivers, went to bed at 3 o'clock and up again 6.30.

9.5.46.

I think I told you, we go out Monday morning 7 a.m. on a scheme and don't come back until 7 p.m. Tuesday. The worst part about it is, we don't get any sleep until Tuesday night. We start off at Warminster and finish at Salisbury so there will be bags of walking to do. It's mostly recce and fighting patrols, there are 2,000 blokes on it and all firing some sort of weapon. That will be our last night scheme then Wednesday and Thursday are written tests. Saturday, I take four squads on drill and in the afternoon I take two lectures on map reading and another on "platoons in attack".

14.5.46.

I've just arrived back from the scheme half an hour ago. I feel dead tired; my poor feet.

Yesterday was marching, running, crawling, swimming through rivers, we covered miles. We cooked our own food in mess tins on a red-hot day and I felt thirsty and hungry.

You needed bags of stamina. The area we were in represented Arnhem in Holland and Jerry had cut our supplies. We weren't allowed to go in shops.

Night came and I was in charge of thirty men to go out on a fighting patrol. We set out at 11 p.m. arriving back at 5 a.m. It took us an hour to go one mile crawling all the way. The object was to blow up a Jerry ammo dump. We succeeded but only after three hours slinging grenades and firing weapons. I'm afraid they take it too seriously because a few blokes were slightly injured. After breakfast we raced across valleys and fields and finally reached our objective (an aerodrome).

It was fun but terribly hard work. I laughed when some of the poor devils fell in the river or ripped their trousers on some barbed wire and yet at times, I could have cried with feeling so tired. While the course is practically over now, it has been glorious in England for one reason only and that's because I've been able to see you.

27.5.46.

(Written upon Ronnie's return from leave in Rochdale)

I'm writing this in the canteen at Victoria Station. When the train left Manchester I went in the lavatory and had a real good cry. It made me feel better. Please thank your father and mother for being so wonderful towards me.

Well, I left off there to catch the 4 p.m. train. I'm writing this in the transit camp at Dover. It took five hours to get here and I had to change three times. So far, I've met four blokes going back to Austria who were on the course. Anyway I've got a bit of company. I don't know what time we leave here tomorrow but if I get a minute I'll write again.

L/Sgt. R.H. Williams
"C" Coy 2nd Battn.
The Loyal Regt.
C.M.F.

28.5.46.

I've just posted a letter to you and I've got three minutes in which to catch the boat but as you can see, I'm now l/ sergeant.

They say it's deadly out there now, guards four nights out of six, but I'll let you know everything when I get back.

28.5.46.

I can only write a couple of lines. It's 8 p.m. and I'm leaving this transit camp in Calais in ten minutes.

I've been sweating cobs carrying all my kit – what a weight.

Will write again as soon as I can. I'm sorry it's so short, darling, but it's better than none: I'm writing this against a wall.

Goodbye my beloved, I love you with all my heart. Goodnight and God bless.

31.5.46.

I've just arrived at Villach in Austria and in a few minutes, I'll be getting on the train to Graz, so I should get back to the Loyals some time tomorrow, Saturday.

It's terribly hot here but I'll get used to it again. I'm certainly glad I've got the worst part of the journey over. I was one of the last to get on the train and there were only three of us in the carriage so we had plenty of room.

I've just been told that I don't leave here until next Thursday. It's terrible I've got to hang about and it makes me feel worse than ever. There's nothing here, just small tents which we sleep in. A train left here for Graz yesterday morning. Fancy, a train only runs there once a week.

3.6.46.

I'm now back with the Loyals. At 11.15 I have to go to see the CO, and he'll tell me the result of my course. After seeing him I go to my company about thirty-five miles from here. I didn't expect to leave Villach transit camp until next Thursday, but we told them we couldn't hang about for a week, so finally they got us a special train to Graz. I got my first stripe on 28th December, and within three months I was sergeant, I can't grumble at that! Now thirty-one groups are going and I hardly know anybody.

I was talking to a bloke at Villach. He said some of these new kids are very stupid and cheeky. Two of them went into Yugoslavia last night and demanded wine from the civilians at the point of a bayonet. Tito's blokes opened up with machine guns and one of the kids was shot, but the other got back. I can see I'll have to be strict with some of them.

I hope you enjoyed the party, and the very best of luck with your play this weekend. I'll be thinking of you on holiday in Filey. Have a good rest.

Well, I left off there to see the CO. The result of my course had just come through and he was very pleased with it. The whole result was "well above average".

I'm in a small village which is a bit better than the last place. I'm writing this in the sergeants' mess. Some civilians used to live here; it's quite a comfortable place and I've got a spring bed too. An Austrian bloke cooks for us and some of our own men clean up for us and so far, I can't grumble. We're right on the Yugoslav border here for patrols and guards. I don't know whether I'll be training the blokes or not yet but I'll soon get to know.

Sgt. R.H.Williams

"C" Coy 2nd Battn.

The Loyal Regt.

C.M.F.

15.7.46.

(This is the first long gap in Ronnie's correspondence. He is returning from leave in England, during which time he and Hilda went to Butlin's at Filey for a week.)

It's so wonderful to think about you, that glorious week at Filey, those heavenly three weeks at home with you. I'll write tomorrow before I go to Calais.

16.7.46.

I don't know when I'll get back to the Loyals, it all depends on how many trains run to Graz. I don't want another week in Villach transit camp.

I realise my job in the army hasn't finished yet so I'll do my best until the end.

Remember me to your mother and father, and thank them for everything, they've been great to me.

17.7.46.

This time I'm writing from Calais transit camp. Since I got here it's been one mad dash, signing papers, getting blankets, etc. I got a hundred cigarettes, a bar of chocolate and two boxes of matches.

Well, I didn't get into trouble for having two days extra. I altered the date on my pass from the 13th to the 15th with an indelible pencil so no one was any the wiser except me of course.[30]

I'll write as soon as I get to Villach.

19.7.46.

Well, here I am at Villach transit camp. I suppose I'll be here for a few days. As I told you before it's deadly but I don't feel so bad this time because it's the last time and each day that passes is one nearer to being with you always.

On the train I pulled my greatcoat from out of my kit bag to sit on and believe it or not the bottom was all covered in wet grass – the greatcoat, I mean. I'd never noticed it before. What glorious memories of Filey.

---

30 Ronnie was obviously desperate to spend an extra couple of days with Hilda, and was very lucky to get away with altering the date on his pass: he would have got into terrible trouble if that had been discovered. Later, on another leave, he altered the dates again to spend a few more days with her, no matter what it cost him.

Some blokes out of the Loyals going on release have just told me the Loyals are now in Vienna. They went there a week ago today. I'm glad I saw them otherwise I'd have gone to Graz. It's fourteen hours on the train from Villach to Vienna.

21.7.46.

(Letter heading: "Church of Scotland Huts – Canteen and St Andrew's Club)

I left Villach last night and I'm writing now from Bruck in a small canteen on the station; it's now 3 a.m. Sunday morning. I should get back to the Loyals tomorrow afternoon.

I feel terribly tired with all this travelling but I should get a few hours' sleep on this train.

21.7.46.

At long last I'm back with the Loyals. We don't wear battledress here but kit like that I wore at home. Our main job here is to do the ceremonial palace guards, but there are other places to guard as well. I won't be doing the quartermaster's job after all; they'd deferred his release for three months until I came back, but he's decided to sign on for another year. However, I don't lose the crown; I'm a staff sergeant instructor, I'm taking drill and guard mountings and get just the same pay as the quartermaster – it's thirteen shillings a day. It's the same rank only a different job, but carry on addressing my letters as sergeant.[31]

It's certainly going to take some settling down to this life after that glorious holiday with you.

---

31 The crown above the three stripes indicated the rank of staff sergeant, so Ronnie has been promoted yet again, a remarkable achievement considering he was still only twenty-two.

I believe we leave Vienna about 15th August and return to somewhere near Graz where we were before, doing patrols on the Yugoslav border, etc. You will be in Scarborough then, won't you, but I'll be thinking of you just the same.

I caught a glance of Vienna coming through in the truck this morning. It's certainly not the same musical Vienna of yesterday and has been scarred by the war. Most buildings have suffered bomb damage, shop windows are boarded up and a dirty, scruffy Russian patrols with a Tommy gun. Instead of being gay it appears tense and weird. The Vienna horse show is on from 24th July to the 26th. I saw some of the horses today doing some exercises – some of them are kept in stables in this barracks. They are beautiful horses and there are competitors from all over the world. I'll go if I get the opportunity.

There's very little room in these barracks but the billets are quite good and you can keep your kit clean. The barracks are on the outskirts of Vienna. You've got to get on two or three trams before you can get to the centre. Quite a number of the blokes say they are always getting lost.

The Period of the Letters

Edith and Wilfred standing outside the shop during the period in which the letters were written.

WILLIAMS-CARTWRIGHT.—The engagement is announced between Ronald, only son of Mrs. and the late Mr. T. H. Williams of 172 Redcross Street N., and Hilda, only daughter of Mr. and Mrs. W. J. Cartwright of 418 Halifax Road, Rochdale.

ROCHDALE OBSERVER.
DEC 22nd 1945

The notice of Hilda and Ronnie's engagement in the Rochdale Observer *on 22nd December 1945.*

*Hilda and Ronnie on
holiday at Butlin's, Filey,
in June 1946.*

*Iris, around the time when
Hilda and Wilfred went
to Ludlow in 1946.*

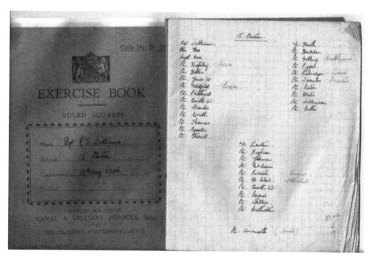

*Details of the platoon Ronnie was in charge of in August 1946
in Austria, written in his meticulous writing.*

Ronnie's clothing coupons for 1946–47.

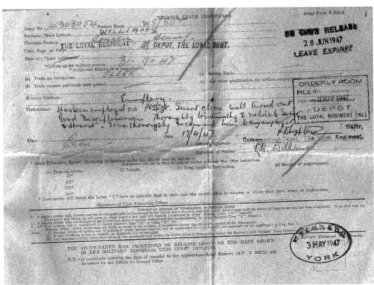

Ronnie's outstanding discharge reference from the army.

The insignia on Ronnie's jacket at the time of his discharge.

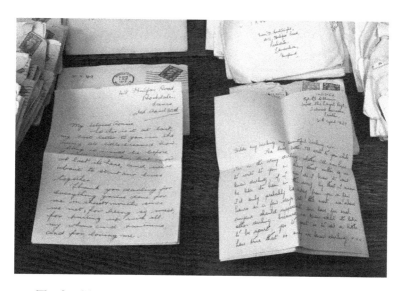

The final letters which Hilda and Ronnie wrote to each other on 30th April 1947, whilst he was waiting to be demobbed at Fulwood Barracks in Preston.

Ronnie's medals and regimental badge.

The letters, also showing the 1940s suitcases in which they are usually kept. The oak table is Ronnie and Hilda's dining table bought from Lovick's in Rochdale when they returned from their honeymoon. Dark red roses were always Hilda's favourite flowers, and were what she had in her wedding bouquet.

⌒℮⌒

As previously mentioned, Hilda's letters written in the first few months of their correspondence were subsequently lost. From this point onwards, all those in italics are hers.

418 Halifax Road
Rochdale
Lancs

15.7.46.

My first letter after your leave. 10.30 at night, and already seems years since you left me.[32] As I saw your bus disappearing, I knew that you'd taken my heart. My heart went with you, keep it safely.

Thank you for a month that I could never forget, for a month of lovely memories.

I've been trying to work hard today to fill in the empty place your going has made in my life. I missed you most when I was on the bus coming to Rochdale after school and I knew you wouldn't be there to meet me.

---

32 Ronnie and Hilda would not see each other for another five and a half months, when Ronnie got his next leave.

16.7.46.

I was going to stay in tonight and knit or read or something but I realised that I couldn't bear to sit alone thinking of all the times you'd been here. So off I went to the Regal by myself. The film was quite good: it was Shock. *You saw the trailer, but how different it seemed with no Ronnie.*

I was wondering how we'll manage the money when we're married. What do you think if we both pool a certain amount of money each week for the housekeeping (including rent, rates, bills, food, etc.), then what we each have left is our own for clothes, buses, amusements, etc. I was even wondering which night in the week I'd go for our rations.

It's the big day for rounders tomorrow. I've had these kids practising a lot, with a hard ball. It's being held on Middleton cricket ground and there are even printed tickets for it. I've sold fifty-four since yesterday afternoon to my own class alone.

We got eighty pairs of PT shoes at school today. I'm so glad because I'm tired of seeing kids trying to run in clogs.

We've had some wonderful times, haven't we? I shall never forget Filey. I'm glad we got those photographs. They are on my dressing table now.

17.7.46.

I suppose you will be well on your way now. I'm thinking of you on the train.

After all the practising of the last few days for rounders we played the finals tonight: we won! We're the top team in Middleton now. They were as nervous as anything before starting, and the other team were confident but as soon as we started everything changed. They are intelligent, they remembered everything and tried hard. I'm awfully pleased with them. The score was 3–0, the same as the last match. Four of us have promised them ice cream for winning. I'm going to ask if we can have a photograph taken to put in the hall along with the winners of the good old 1920s. I had to umpire again. Even in the finals they couldn't find anybody willing to be a neutral umpire in all Middleton schools.

I went to the same cafe that we went to for my tea. I sat at the table and I felt so lonely without you.

Pop says I have to tell you that one of his hens has died, and mother sends her love. She brought me an ashtray and a cute little green dog back from Llangollen.

Pop's bike has just got a puncture. He says you wouldn't be able to use it tonight if you were here!

23.7.46.

I'm writing this in the guard room, myself and twenty-four men in charge of nine prisoners. What prisoners they are; four of them have tried to break out today.

About a week ago there was a big dance in Vienna. Some Russian officers went into the dance and started knocking the women about. I believe there was nearly a whole battalion of the Argyll Scottish Highlanders in the dance so a real fight started. The British troops dragged the Russians outside and threw them over a bridge, five Russians died with crushed skulls and one British soldier was shot. Two of the men who were seen during the fight are in this prison now awaiting trial. I believe that's how it is in Vienna every night; no one seems to like the Russians. I haven't been into Vienna yet.

I said we would move from Vienna about 15th August but it's been changed since to the 10th. It will take about seven hours from Vienna to Graz but that's a short journey considering what I've done this past week.

Thank you from the bottom of my heart for the three letters I received today. I think that's a good idea to pool our money when we're married. I'll buy my own clothes but I'd give you most of my money because you will need more than I will for clothes. I don't drink and my clothes will last me ages. We'll manage all right.

I'm so proud of you and the kids for winning the rounders final. They certainly deserved an ice cream each.

It's lights out in this barracks at 10.15, so when I'm not on guard I'm always in bed early and always up at 6.

18.7.46.

This is good going, I have managed a letter every day so far. It's my only compensation for missing you. Everything was all right at school today. I'm now training the kids for the inter-school swimming gala next week. I'm taking some of them down to the baths at 4 o'clock tomorrow.

Let me know soon as you can what I have to address you as – staff sergeant or what?

Marjorie has gone out with Tom again tonight – the twenty-sixth consecutive night by my reckoning. I hope to goodness she doesn't bring him back again tonight. They were here last night whispering and giggling, leaving us to get the supper ready. It's not fair, is it?

I was thinking about Australia today. If you got the job would you have to do a lot of travelling? Should I be able to travel with you?[33]

I feel so restless tonight. You know how it is – that feeling that you can't settle down to anything and at the same time it's too much trouble to go out and the evening stretches like a vast eternity before you.

---

33 This would appear to have been a job opportunity from Robinson's. It seems that in the end nothing came of it.

25.7.46.

Thanks once again for another beautiful letter. It was so sweet of you to write when Tom and Marjorie[34] were there; fancy twenty-six consecutive nights out. No, it isn't fair they should leave you and your mother to get the meal ready every time. Let them do it themselves.

This last few days the weather has been glorious, red hot sunshine.

If I got the job in Australia, I don't know whether I'd travel or not, however I'm writing to Robinson's next week and when I get the reply, I'll let you know.

Last night I went into Vienna, my first night out since I left home. I jumped off the tram and slipped and sprained my left wrist rather badly. I didn't feel it at first until it started to swell up. I didn't feel like walking about, most of the shops were closed and all I could see were dirty, scruffy Russians carrying rifles. Vienna is awful; civilians starving; like most European countries the place is full of prostitutes.

I went to the hospital for an X-ray but nothing was broken, it's just a sprain. I've got a tight bandage on now and it feels

---

34 Marjorie, three years older than Hilda, was another of her cousins, the daughter of Edith's eldest sister Clara. Marjorie had had a very difficult time since when she was sixteen, her father had left home and her mother committed suicide. It was Marjorie who found Clara when she came home from school. After that, and with many other problems along the way, Marjorie stayed for a lot of the time either with Hilda's parents or with the parents of her other cousin Bill. Marjorie got married to her boyfriend Tom early in 1947, and it sounds as though at this time, yet again, she had nowhere to go and things were getting a bit strained for Hilda and her parents: two young women in their twenties, each waiting to get married, were forced to share a bed because there was no spare room. Otherwise, Marjorie and Hilda had always been close, and they later got over their differences; Marjorie was extremely kind to Hilda's mother Edith in her old age.

much better. Anyway, it's taught me a lesson never to jump off a running tram.

20.7.46.

It's Saturday night and I'm alone in the house. This time last week we were holding hands in the Queen's, Littleborough. Remember how we queued for an ice cream and didn't get any? Remember our picnic to Blackstone Edge?

I went to the pictures by myself tonight, to the Empire to see The Captive Heart, *a story about men in a German prison camp. It was quite well done, and more than once I had a lump in my throat when I thought that it might have been you.*

Last night I took some of the girls for a swimming practice after school then went to Littleborough pictures with my mother. For once she didn't go to sleep. The film was the one we thought we should see last Saturday, Within these Walls, *and we enjoyed it. We took an apple and an orange each, but we only managed the apple. We thought the scent of the orange might be a little too overpowering.*

I got your letter from Calais yesterday. I suppose now you'll either be at Villach, on your way to Graz, or maybe even Vienna.

Someone is knocking at the door now, some late customer, but I shan't go. I won't give up one of these precious moments of writing to you.

27.7.46.

Saturday afternoon 3.15. At 4.30 I'm taking some prisoners to the palace jail, and then I mount the palace guard so I will be late back tonight. A fortnight today we went on the picnic to Blackstone Edge.[35] It seems ages since then.

---

35 The beginning of the moors beyond Littleborough and on the way to Yorkshire, a wild and spectacular landscape.

I miss you terribly but every second I think of you. I even think of you Saturday mornings having a bath in the cellar!

22.7.46.

What a busy day it's been. I came home from school today and had to do some work all evening because my mother was so tired with the bread rationing starting today.[36] I've been ironing mostly. Tomorrow night I shall be working again because my mother goes to Scarborough and Marjorie wants to go to the pictures with Tom. Still, better that than sitting here with them all evening.

I find it hard to talk about ordinary things, yet I must. Our boys won the shield at the swimming gala today.

I had a letter from your mother today asking me to go to tea on Sunday, so if you get this letter in time do think of me there. Remember how nervous I was the first time I went?

23.7.46.

Once again, just me and my lamp. I've closed the shop, done some washing and mending, been to the library and here I am.

I'm looking forward to hearing from Austria soon: I want to know how your journey was and that you are safely settled down again.

I found some wonderful howlers in 1b's history test. Did you know that Captain Cook discovered the North and South Poles? (Simultaneously, I presume.) And that the Roundheads fought in the Battle of the Nile? And that the French Revolution began in 1733 and ended in 1921? And that the Civil War was the Silver War, and

---

36 This was a new form of rationing introduced by the Labour Government because continual rain had ruined the wheat crop. It lasted for two years, and was considered to be the height of austerity.

that Nelson and Washington fought at Waterloo, and that George XVI existed? Aren't they just wonderful?

I've just heard I'm to have 1a next year. It may come to nothing but there's a sporting chance. At least there might not be quite so many dopes in an A class. But I like the little duffers all the same.

The other night I dreamed that my Auntie Emily[37] *had left me £3,000 and I was just going to buy a house with it when Pop woke me up. See how my mind runs even in my sleep?*

29.7.46.

I'm writing this in the company office, it's 9.30 p.m. and everyone else has gone out or is on guard. It's just started to rain, the first time since I came back. There's a wireless in this office. I've had it on all evening. There's a recording on of *Tales from the Vienna Woods*. It's beautiful. Music like that seems to bring me closer to you.

As I write this, I'm smoking your pipe. It's a beautiful pipe, because it doesn't burn your tongue and you gave it to me.

I've been battalion orderly sergeant today. My feet ache with walking about and the terrific heat from the sun hasn't helped. I drilled some blokes in the barrack square for an hour this afternoon and the sweat rolled off me. It's a wonder we didn't all faint. Last night I took some more prisoners to the palace jail. They were British soldiers who deserted. We went past the Danube coming back so at least I've seen something in Vienna. It looked lovely with the moon shining on it. Just before I got back a great wind came up. It was so strong there were broken windows all over the barracks this morning. Blokes who had left their clothes out to dry just couldn't find them and I suppose some Austrians did well for themselves.

---

37   Emily (Hilda's mother's surviving sister) and her husband, Jesse, were the parents of Bill.

I hope the girls win the swimming at school. I wish them lots of luck. I hope you enjoyed your tea at Mother's yesterday. She likes you very much, I knew she would. Yes, I remember how nervous you were the first time you called.

Perhaps by the time you get this letter it will be your birthday. I've asked the blokes if they can get anything in Vienna but there isn't a thing so I'm enclosing a £1 note. I didn't change it at Calais. It will do for the pictures or anything. I couldn't even get a birthday card. This is the first birthday you've had since I met you and I wish you very, very many happy returns of the day on 4ᵗʰ August.

26.7.46.

Tonight I got your first letter from Vienna and the one before it. Thank you a thousand times for them.

We had some terrific thunderstorms this afternoon and the rain was coming down in torrents. I had to wait about forty minutes before I could leave school. I was so wet that I even had to change my underwear when I got home.

Are you sorry you haven't got the quartermaster's job? I'm not, if it has saved your release being deferred by three months. Why can't I address you as staff sergeant yet?

Marjorie has Valerie here for the weekend. Mrs Lord came with her today.[38] Much squawking and squealing and crying. Shades of bedlam! But it's quieter now.

I'm going swimming tomorrow with Audrey. It's her mother who's making that new cherry-red linen dress for me.[39] I've been for a fitting tonight. I think it's going to be nice.

---

38 Valerie was Marjorie's daughter born in 1941, the result of an affair Marjorie had with a married man. Because of the stigma of illegitimacy at the time, Marjorie had Valerie cared for by a foster mother, Mrs Lord, until Marjorie got married to her boyfriend Tom in 1947 and was able to take Valerie back.

39 It was quite common at the time to have clothes made by a tailor.

I'm going to make my mother's supper now because she's tired and wants to go to bed.

31.7.46.

It's 9.45 p.m. and I've got just half an hour to write this before lights out. The reason I'm so late is because I've just arrived from Graz. I had to go and fetch the advance party of the East Yorkshire Regiment; they are taking over our guards in Vienna. I was up at 5.30 so I'm feeling a little tired.

I'm trying to think what our house will be like. At least we've got a few things for it. I know we can't do much until I come home. I wonder what we'll be doing this time next year?

2.8.46.

It's 6 p.m. Friday. Tonight I'm on my way to Graz once more. This time I'm going to fetch some Austrians who are supposed to be pro-Nazi. I'm bringing them back to Vienna for the trial which opens 5th August.

This will be a short letter because we have to cross the Russian zone before 8 o'clock. After that time there may be some shooting. 8 o'clock is the curfew for the Russian zone and we have passes printed in Russian, but half of them can't read.

29.7.46.

Your letters from Vienna are coming regularly now. As you can see, I have enclosed two photographs. What do you think of them?

I went to your house yesterday and had a very nice time.

I've been busy tonight. I let my mother and dad go to the pictures together, looked after the shop and did some ironing.[40] *The only things I didn't iron were Marjorie's because I don't see why I should do her work instead of writing to you when she's out. It's just the principle of not undertaking her responsibilities. It's the least she can do to iron them when my mother even washes them all for £1 a week (including Tom's meals).*

Don't think me silly when I suggest this, but couldn't we have some definite time each day when we think of nothing else but each other so that it seems as though we are making a telephone call on a sort of emotional wavelength? How about 10 p.m.? As soon as you get this letter you will know that every day at that time, I'm thinking of you.

Today at the chemist's I got a bottle of Coty foundation lotion. You put it on before you put powder on and it smells and feels heavenly. All the same, I saved £3 10s. out of my last month's salary. I guess there won't be much chance of saving next month but I'll do my best.

I had one awkward customer in tonight. He came in and asked for cigarettes. I told him we hadn't got any and a moment or two later he came back again still asking for cigarettes. He began to turn nasty, you know the style: "It's not right… etc.", when, to his great surprise, not worrying about the customer always being right, I turned the rough edge of my schoolma'am's tongue on him and expounded upon the problems shopkeepers have already without being worried about cigarettes. He went out rather meekly.

I've washed that little coat that you like, it's come out quite nice again. One of these days when you're home, and if ever we have the money, I'll buy a white coat because I'm sure that's what you'd like to see me in.

(On the same date, Hilda also sent a short note with a parcel in which she had included a cake she made herself, shoelaces, razor blades and a book of poetry.)

---

40   Having a shop which opened early morning and closed at 10 o'clock at night meant that Hilda's parents were scarcely ever able to go out together in the evening.

1.8.46.

You do need me to hold your hand (and I think your hands are beautiful) when you go jumping off trams and spraining your wrist! Take care of it.

We have a day's holiday on Monday for Bank Holiday and break up on Wednesday until September. On the last afternoon we're having dancing displays by some of the girls and on Tuesday afternoon having a rounders match, staff versus team. We're all playing except Miss Taylor and Miss Hobson who say they're getting too old for it, so they'll umpire. I've decided to have my hair done again, not at Hawarth's[41] but a little place not far from here at Hurstead.

All the kids know my birthday is on Sunday, and they have been pestering me for my address. This time last year I was in a flat spin getting ready for my twenty-first.

Tomorrow at school I'm taking a Greek dancing lesson for the first time there, wearing my Greek dancing dress of course. A student teacher is going to play the piano for me. I was playing the piano at dinnertime, a Chopin prelude, and Gibby[42] came in and insisted that I played it again for him. I must be improving.[43]

I shall probably go to Ludlow[44] with Pop at the end of August and I think my granny and my little cousin Iris from Birmingham will go too. We love going there. I don't know yet where we shall

---

41 Hawarth's was a little department store in the Esplanade in Rochdale town centre where people used to go for their finer clothing, household goods, etc.

42 Mr Gibson, the headmaster.

43 Hilda had piano lessons throughout her days at Bury Grammar School, her parents having bought her a new piano in 1936 for use at home.

44 On one occasion when Hilda was thirteen, her father had taken her to Ludlow to help her get over a terrible tragedy. She had been on holiday in Morecambe with some friends slightly older than herself. Hilda and two of her friends were swept out to sea by the unexpectedly powerful current; Hilda saved one of the girls and herself, but her other friend drowned.

stay but it may be with my Great-Aunt Jinnie. We'll have to go to Ludlow together some time. I think you would like it. When I was quite a young girl, I was walking on Whitcliffe Hill[45] outside the walls one night, looking over the river to the castle in the town and there was a moon coming out; everything was peaceful and lovely. I felt more at home there than in any place I know and I decided (at the tender age of thirteen) that if I ever fell in love, I should take my lover there because only he would be able to share it with me and make it more beautiful.

I sent you a little parcel the other night.

S. Sgt. R.H. Williams
"C" Coy 2nd Battn.
The Loyal Regt.
C.M.F.

4.8.46.

I got the swimming trunks I ordered before I went on leave, they are blue wool and very nice too. I went swimming this afternoon, the first time since I came back. It was a glorious day. The open-air bath is in another barracks ten minutes' walk from ours and the water was lovely and warm. I'm not very good at diving: I dived from the twenty-foot board and hit the water like a pancake. I thought I'd split my stomach open.

I've decided I'm going to learn tennis properly, not out here but when I come home. I think I've played most sports so I want to play tennis too. When you see Bill, ask him to save the tennis racket and I'll buy it from him when I come home.[46]

---

45 Whitcliffe Common, an area of fifty-two acres, is immediately to the south of Ludlow, above which it rises. It gives outstanding views of the town, the castle, St Laurence Church and the Clee Hills.

46 Hilda herself taught Ronnie to play tennis when he was demobbed, and they continued to play for many years.

The reason I didn't put staff sergeant on my previous letters was because you've got to hold the rank for twenty-one days before you can do that. I've got all that backpay now. I'm the only staff sergeant instructor in the battalion.

Our next place is a village called Fürstenfeld. There I'll be instructing practically every bloke in the battalion on weapon training and field craft, so I'm going to be busy. I've got to make reports on every man, his progress, character and discipline.

I've spent very little money since I came back. I sent £2 home to Mother the other day. I realise you can't save anything this month with going to Scarborough and perhaps on holiday with your father. Please don't worry about saving.

Well, darling, you're twenty-two today, once again I wish you very, very many happy returns of the day. I only wish we could have spent it together.

I think that is a terrific idea thinking about each other at 10 o'clock every night. It will be 10 o'clock by your time and 11 o'clock by my time. I think it's another way of bringing us as close together as we can be while we're apart.

I laughed about 3 o'clock this morning. I know it's a queer time to laugh but I got into bed at 10 o'clock and the two sergeants in my room started to talk about football. It went on till 12 o'clock. I must've fallen off to sleep talking about it because I jumped up about 3 o'clock yelling: "Shoot!! Send him off, ref!" I had to laugh when they woke me up.

6.8.46.

(Re-addressed to Hilda, by then on a course in Scarborough)

I thought of you at 11 o'clock last night, knowing you were thinking of me at the same time.

It's 5.10 p.m. and at 5.30 I've got to go to the palace and hand over the guards to the East Yorkshire Regiment. That's the first guard they've taken over so far, and our last guard will be handed over on the 9th. I should finish the changing over about 7 p.m., so after that I'm going to spend the rest of the evening looking round Vienna to see if there's anything I can buy for you.

Yesterday, Lieutenant General Steele commanding British troops in Austria came to the battalion.[47] Myself and the three smartest privates in the battalion formed a guard of honour. When he inspected us, he said to me "You're the smartest NCO I've seen during my tour in Austria". He asked me if I was signing on and I said: "No sir, I've got a beautiful wife waiting for me".

This morning it appeared on battalion orders: "Commanding Officer wishes to congratulate Staff Sergeant Williams R.H. on a very outstanding turn-out".

By the time you get this letter you will be in Scarborough. I hope you enjoy it; do look after yourself. I'm certainly glad I went there with you as I know where you're staying so I can imagine what everything is like. I hope you have plenty of sunny weather.

3.8.46.

In a few minutes it will be August 4th and I'll be twenty-two. I shan't be able to get used to not being twenty-one any longer.

I do wish with all my heart that you could be with me for my birthday, although it's not that it will be anything special, unlike last year.

---

47 James Steele became a lieutenant general in 1946. He was appointed commander-in-chief and high commissioner in Austria in 1946: in that capacity he signed a treaty with Marshal Tito. He was promoted to general in 1947. He was adjutant-general to the forces from 1947 to 1950, when he retired from the British Army, and became aide-de-camp general to the King.

Last year there were about seventy-five people and what a day it was![48] *There were so many things to do and so many people here I didn't even have time to eat. The only drink I had was one glass of sherry when we were drinking a toast. I've never seen our house with so many people in it. When we came back from the club there were at least thirty people here, and more standing outside. I danced, I talked, I organised games. I got up at 6 in the morning and went to bed at 5 the following morning. Although I was really in the limelight, I didn't have a thousandth of the happiness it gives me just to be able to write to you and think of you.*

My mother will be in Scarborough for my second week there, not in the same place, but quite near, so that will be all right.

Today I wrote to the Feathers Hotel in Ludlow to see what their terms are, because there won't be enough room for us all at Great-Aunt Jinnie's. It's a lovely hotel, it's really old, and Pop will pay for me if we stay there.

8.8.46.

Well, I had a look round Vienna last night, I walked miles but couldn't get any perfume, silk stockings, etc., but I managed to get some lipstick and powder from the sergeants' canteen. They are sending it on for me. I gave them your address. When I get to our new billet I'll try to get into Graz and see if I can buy anything there. Most of the shops were shut, so I went to the pictures for the first time since I came back; Boris Karloff in *Bedlam* set during the seventeenth century, about the treatment and horrors of the asylum. I enjoyed it if only for the rest. I felt terribly lonely on my own.

---

48 The "club" referred to, was a place called the Egerton Club within walking distance of the shop. Hilda's twenty-first birthday seems to have been an extraordinarily grand occasion considering that her parents were not wealthy, just a very hard-working baker and owners of a small shop. The Egerton Club was basically a large hall available for hire. Years later Hilda and Ronnie would play badminton there in the local league.

I do hope you enjoy it in Ludlow, I'm sure you will. Tell your dad I hope he enjoys it. I'd love to go there with you.

By the time you get this letter I should be settled down in my new surroundings, and I'll let you know what I'm doing and what the place is like.

6.8.46.

How can I ever thank you for being so sweet and thoughtful about my birthday? I promise I'll let you know exactly what I do with the pound.

I'm tired, I guess it's that end-of-term feeling. There have been all the reports to make out, after marking all the exams, etc. and so many things to clear up. Only one more day now and my holiday begins.

I did my packing after tea because my luggage goes in advance tomorrow. I spent Monday night ironing and mending things, but I don't mind being busy when you're away. I'm so glad your wrist is better. I hope you will have managed to see a bit more of Vienna before you leave it.

I kept on wishing you were going to Scarborough with me.[49] At last I got the new dress that was being made for me. I do think you would like it. Think of me in Scarborough, thinking of you.

10.8.46.

I'm now in my new billet which is quite good. From the outside the place looks like a large hotel. I'm in a room on my own with a spring bed, table and chair, but nothing like home, of course.

It's rather a big village, but very quiet, no entertainment, a swimming pool about a mile away. That's all I can say about the place so far.

---

49   Hilda was going on a course there.

How can I thank you for the parcel, for the chewing gum, and the cake which is smashing? I notice in your letter you made the cake yourself; you can certainly bake!

I shall be looking forward to seeing your new class when I come home, although some of them will probably have seen me before.

Yesterday morning I'd nothing to do so I went into Vienna and had my dinner. While I was sitting there, I heard some sergeants say, "There's a dozen pairs of stockings just come in at the welfare centre". I flew out of the canteen and fate was with me. I managed to get you two pairs of fully fashioned, size 9. It was lucky I had a duty-free label with me so you won't have to pay tax this time. The welfare will post them because you're not allowed to bring them out.

12.8.46.

I've been awfully busy today making an assault course. You should have seen me up in the trees tying ropes. What weather we're having; it's so hot I sweat even if I'm sitting down. Bags of mosquitoes here, some of the blokes are full of bites. I've escaped them so far.

Yes, I thought of you on your birthday. I wished with all my heart I could have been with you. Yes, I even thought about last year when all those people were at your birthday.

8.8.46.

Only one more day and then I go to Scarborough. Tomorrow I shall go to the hairdresser's in the afternoon and in the evening press and pack the rest of my things.

I went to Annie's for my tea and spent the evening there. It was a nice change. Annie and I had a good talk about things in general.

We decided that someday we'll both go for a Turkish bath. We talked about having children and such things. Somehow, I don't see how a marriage can really be a marriage without a baby. I love to think that someday I'll be your wife and have yours.

I shall be thinking of you moving from Vienna on Saturday. Maybe by now you will have my parcel. I hope so because I don't want the cake to be too old when you get it.

I think that now Pop is really looking forward to going to Ludlow and staying at the Feathers. My granny is there now because my Great-Aunt Jinnie is ill.

It's a long time since I've seen them. I'll be able to tell them all about you. Pop and I are going to collect as much fruit as we can. We shall try to hire bicycles too, and maybe we'll go on the river. I know I shall go in the castle. It's a very historical place, you know. All the troubles with the barons of the Welsh border started there. It's so near Wales that the people have a Welsh accent.

Scarborough

10.8.46.

I'm writing this on my first night in Scarborough. The train was terribly late here. It was the 9.23 from Rochdale and it didn't arrive until 3.30, over six hours. I was sitting on my case in the corridor all the time except for the last few minutes from Filey to Scarborough. When we were getting near Filey I thought of that truly wonderful week we had there.

This place seems very nice so far. I have a single room. I don't go to lectures until Monday.

I went to the pictures tonight by myself to see The Bells of Saint Mary's, *not bad at all.*

You know Pop and I were planning to stay at the Feathers in Ludlow? Well, I had a letter yesterday to say that they are full so I don't know where we'll stay now.

It does seem funny being here alone. Everywhere I go I bump into some recollection of my college life here. I look at Oliver's Mount, and think of my first geography lecture here when old Joe Push, without a word, led us to the top of it before delivering his lectures. I see a cake shop and think of the times we bought doughnuts. I see the harbour, and I see myself walking along there with Betty one wild, stormy afternoon talking about poetry and music. I passed the Royal Hotel where we used to dance for 1s. 6d where the price is now 5s. at least.[50] I see the lights and remember how we stumbled along between barbed wire in the blackout. And I see holidaymakers and cars where I used to see NAAFIs, soldiers, airmen, tanks and lorries. It's changed a lot since those college days, but I guess I shall always go round corners and find myself bumping into ghosts; happy ghosts. I shall always like the place.

You asked me where we should go for our holidays next year. I don't know, I think I'd like to go somewhere I've never been yet. Do you think we could afford Cornwall or somewhere like that?[51]

15.8.46.

I haven't been very busy today. I finished the assault course this morning, so I went swimming this afternoon: it was lovely and cool in the water. I'm so brown with the hot weather but I suppose it will have worn off by the time I come home.

---

50 It was in fact only two years since Hilda left college in 1944. The increase in price is perhaps because Scarborough was now a holiday resort once more, rather than a place for evacuation and near where large numbers of the armed forces were stationed.

51 They did not go to Cornwall on their honeymoon, but they did go to Newquay on holiday in 1948. They were always adventurous: in 1949 they took the brave step of travelling to Paris by train and boat to visit Hilda's friend Jacques Bonroy and his wife Claire. Hilda got to know Jacques during the war when he was in the Free French Army, stationed in Manchester at the time. A request appeared in the local paper to take in a French soldier over Christmas. Hilda had studied French at school, and she and her parents volunteered to accept someone, who turned out to be Jacques. They remained friends for life.

Last night I played football even though it was far too hot. We lost two goals to one against the Hampshire Regiment. The sweat just poured off me. This morning I also did a bit of instructing on weapons.

I'm glad you like the place you're staying at in Scarborough. I can just see you sitting in the lounge writing your letters. Enjoy the course. I'm glad it's in Scarborough because you spent two important years there, gay and happy, and that's how I always want you to be.

Part of this building was full of old papers and documents, so today some of the lads cleaned the place out. There were letters dating back to 1865. Some of the stamps I enclose were off the letters, I thought perhaps you'd like them. One document I noticed was signed by Eva Braun and another by Hitler.

This village is on the Austrian/Hungarian border. Half a mile away are the Russians. I believe this lot aren't too bad; the Mongolians are the worst.

18.8.46.

2 a.m. Sunday. I was going to write tonight but I shan't be able to. At 2.30 a.m. I'm going out on patrol to a village sixty miles from here called Gleisdorf on the Hungarian border. There have been reports of pro-Nazis living in the village so myself and fifteen men are allotted the task of sorting them out.

You know I've never settled down since I came back to Austria. All I can think about is civvy street. If I were making the army my career it would be different but all I want to do is get back, settle down, get married and do a sensible job. You're not free in the army. At least you get weekends off, you can go where you like. When I'm back we'll be able to do things together, make our own little plans. Another reason why I'm fed up with the army is because I've no real friends now, they've all gone on release and friends mean everything in the army.

The reason your mail was only taking three days to come was because it now comes by air three times a week instead of by rail from Calais. I suppose odd letters will still come that way.

12.8.46.

When I got your letter this teatime telling me what the general said to you I was so proud I could have burst with pride. I know that you deserved his congratulations because I know how smart you always look. Now do you wonder why I suggested you should get married in your uniform?

A very nice thing happened to me this morning. I was having coffee and a sandwich at break this morning when who should come up to me but Nancy, my college friend and her sister, Rosalind. I went out with them tonight to the Opera House to see The Young Mrs Barrington *and I shall see them again tomorrow. They live in Wellington in Shropshire so when I'm in Ludlow they've invited me to go over for a day.*

I think I shall like the course. My part of it is mostly at the girls' high school where we used to play netball, though tomorrow we go to the boys' high school as well to see a demonstration of some apparatus and to have a photograph taken. I've met one or two people who were on the course in Blackpool at Easter. Remember how cold and crowded it was? But it was worth it just to be with you.

20.8.46.

(Redirected to the Feathers Hotel, Ludlow)

As I told you, there's no entertainment here, so since I'm sports organiser for the battalion I'm getting things cracking.

Yesterday I made a netball pitch with nets, etc. The blokes can't leave it alone now, they were on it all afternoon. It was anything but netball, more like rugby! I think everybody's shirt was ripped by the time the game finished. The score was 19-17. This afternoon I made a volleyball pitch. Since this company is the biggest in the battalion, it's done very well for sports equipment. So far, I've got four footballs, three cricket bats, four cricket balls, two handballs, nets, mats, and medicine balls. That's what the blokes want, bags of sport. The trouble is lately they've had all work and no play which doesn't go down well.

I have to find some indoor games for the dark nights: table tennis, darts, cards, etc. They have a canteen and get plenty of beer, but of course sergeants aren't allowed in it. As I told you I never go in the sergeants' mess except for meals. I've had one pint of beer since I came back.

By the time you receive this letter you will have finished your course at Scarborough, I do hope you've enjoyed it. I'll be thinking of you in Ludlow with your dad. I know you'll enjoy being there with him. I like your father very much. There aren't many like him; you can talk to him, he knows what it's like to be in the army and rough it. Your mother is great too. I wish I could wash the pots for her now. I always felt very much at home because they made me so welcome.

14.8.46.

The course is pretty strenuous – dancing of all sorts, games, films, swimming and lectures, but I like it. We're even going to do ballroom dancing. We do folk dancing, national character dancing, even a bit of Greek and modern thrown in.

I'm really glad you want to learn tennis. I'm sure you'd like it if we go at it a little more slowly to start with, but we couldn't expect to make a Wimbledon player of you in one hour. There's a lot of technique and footwork to master in tennis, and I think given time you'd like it.

Today was the nicest day we've had so far, sunshine all day. This afternoon we went swimming. It was grand, even though the water was cold. I'd like to see you in your new swimming trunks.

I had a letter from home this morning. Pop was warning me about eating ice cream because of the typhoid that is going round, but I haven't had any here so far.[52]

22.8.46.

I've only got a few minutes in which to write this letter. They've just told me I've got to go to battalion headquarters and collect some extra sports kit. What a stupid time to go, 9 o'clock at night. These things seem to crop up just when I think I've got a couple of hours to myself. When I do get any spare time, most of it I spend writing letters to you and the rest of the time I spend washing my clothes. In this climate you've got to look after yourself. I have a shower every day, it doesn't matter how late night it is, and I change my underclothes every day. It's such a sticky heat it makes you feel very tired.

I'm glad you found some nice friends on the course. I like it when you tell me where you've been because somehow, I can just imagine what the place is like and I feel so much closer to you.

I've got at least half a dozen letters to write to other units stationed in Austria, asking them for fixtures for the cricket, netball, football and volleyball leagues which start this week, oh and hockey too. Besides all that, I've got to make invoices out

---

52 On 5th August the *Daily Express* reported that ice cream had been officially established as the source of an epidemic of typhoid fever in Aberystwyth. "With fourteen new cases yesterday, fifty-seven persons, aged from three to twenty, are at present in hospital. A check following the first six cases showed that they had all bought ice cream from a vendor who had previously had typhoid".

for all the kit, then I've got to go and see the Bürgermeister to try and get the ground. I've plenty of work with sports alone never mind the infantry instructing I've got to do.

17.8.46.

Thank you from the bottom of my heart for the three letters my mother brought today, the photographs and the parcel. My mother didn't bring the parcel because she hadn't room, but she's told me about it. It was falling to pieces, and one box of powder covered the postman with powder, but apart from that it's all right. She brought me the lipstick and it's lovely. I must thank you too for the stockings that are coming.

This morning we had some sports with about ten events: long jump, netball shooting, tennis serving, relay races... There was even dribbling at football. It was grand fun.

4.8.46.

I had a reply from Robinson's yesterday; the director who went to Australia hasn't arrived there yet so they can't tell me anything until he writes. They'll let me know as soon as possible.

I wrote to Auntie Minnie in Australia the other day and asked what it's like out there, what jobs there are, etc.

19.8.46.

What do you think about Cornwall for our honeymoon? I've never been there. If we went there, we should need a whole day for travelling, shouldn't we?

My mother says she has had a bright idea. If we don't get a house straight away, some of the people in one of her houses might

be moving out in a few months so she says we could have it. It's only
small, one up and one down, but it's quite nice, and it would put
us on.[53] *But that's not all. We've got a very good chance of having a*
bathroom and kitchen built onto our house at home so we could have
baths there.[54] *We shouldn't need much furniture either.*[55] *The people*
who live there now will have to move soon because there's just one
bedroom and they're getting too old to sleep in the same room.

26.8.46.

It's 5.15 p.m. and I'm writing this sitting on a milestone near
a village called Spielfeld. The reason is I've been on patrol to
the village and am now waiting for a truck to take me back. It
should be here in about half an hour, but it will be late when I
get back tonight as the camp is sixty-three miles from here. The
wind keeps trying to blow the paper away. I've certainly written
letters in some queer places to you.

We played a football match against the locals yesterday. The
Austrians are very keen on handball, the women too. I saw them
play yesterday and they are quite good at it; same rules as netball
but using football goals instead of the nets.

That will be wonderful if we can have that house your

---

53 "Put us on" means that they could make do with that until something
better came along. It was a common local expression.

54 After getting married, they did indeed go to live in one of Hilda's
parents' properties, but not this one. They finally moved into a back-
to-back cottage on the main road at 424 Halifax Road, and would
remain there until 1954 when they got a council house. That cottage
also consisted of one room upstairs with no bathroom and one room
downstairs with a tiny scullery. To get to the outside toilet meant going
three doors down along the main road, down the side of Hilda's parents'
shop and round the back. The fact that Hilda's parents by then had their
bathroom and indoor toilet installed along the way was an absolute
godsend.

55 The wooden "utility" furniture which Hilda and Ronnie got with their
coupons was so sturdy that it is still in use now.

mother spoke about, it will certainly put us on, and we wouldn't have to wait as long before we got married.

I left most of your old letters at home, but I've got another pile of them now.[56]

22.8.46.

I seem to have been waiting ages for an opportunity to write to you. Things are such a terrible rush. With being at lectures all morning and having lunch late, the afternoon is gone in a flash, and I have been seeing my mother in all my spare time. I was going to write this afternoon but my auntie and uncle came for the day. I think my mother is enjoying her holiday.

Tomorrow morning we go over all the dances we've learned (about twenty-five) and finish up with sports. It's all been very interesting this fortnight, but I guess I'll need the next week in Ludlow to recuperate.

29.8.46.

Thank you again for another wonderful letter. Don't worry if you can't always write to me when you'd like to. I realise you've been terribly busy at Scarborough and you've so many things to attend to.

I feel more tired tonight than I've ever been since I've been in the army. That's saying a lot but the reason is this morning I ran nine miles in the battalion cross-country run and came second. This afternoon I played football against "A" Company; we won two goals to one. I scored both the goals and really felt in form, but the sun was blazing hot, my football boots were too

---

56 These are presumably the letters written by Hilda which are now missing, going from December 1945 to July 1946.

tight and they ripped the skin off my toes. I can hardly walk now, my muscles are so stiff. I suppose it was too much for one day especially in this heat. I'm supposed to be playing football against the locals again tomorrow but I won't be playing, I'll take it easy tomorrow.

This week I've been out every day taking the blokes on training. It's hard work when you're at it every night until 9 o'clock; running about and being in the open air makes you tired.

I suppose you're now at Ludlow with your father. I know you'll enjoy it there. I suppose you'll find it quiet after the bustle of Scarborough, however it will be rest for you and you certainly need it after all that dancing, PT, swimming, etc.

It doesn't matter to me if you are broke, there are times and places where you've got to spend more than usual. I always want you to be happy. I'll save as much as I can while I'm out here, so don't be afraid to spend.

418 Halifax Road
Rochdale
Lancs

24.8.46.

Back home again now, I've survived the course and got the certificate. I've got your two parcels now and I want to thank you from the bottom of my heart. The creams are lovely. I've been using the lipstick which my mother brought, all week. One of the boxes of powder is quite safe, it was just the talcum powder that burst and covered the postman. And the stockings are divine.

I can understand about your not feeling settled down. In a way I'm glad because it means your heart is not there. Is that selfish of me? Sometimes I think I do like my own way a little bit too much.

I had some rather sad news yesterday when I got home. Joe died yesterday morning.[57] He ate a mouse on Wednesday that had eaten some Rodine and had been ill since then. It makes me think I shall never allow myself to get fond of a pet again but I always do. I feel for them terribly when anything happens to them.

Pop and I still don't know where we're going to stay in Ludlow, but I guess we'll find somewhere.

31.8.46.

I suppose by now you will have had your holiday at Ludlow and be home again.

About a week tomorrow I suppose you'll be starting school, am I right? I bet it will take the first week before you get used to it again especially after a long holiday.

I do hope I get the job in Australia because I'm sure I'd never stick working in an office all day. This last four years I've spent every bit of it in the open air. I'd die of suffocation in an office now. We'll just have to see what happens.[58]

My stiffness has worn off and yesterday I played football again against the locals; this time we won five goals to four, but as usual the game was full of fouls and one player was sent off from both sides. I've got a lovely cut on my leg where somebody stuck their boot in me.

This morning I took four Yugoslav prisoners to a jail on the Hungarian border. I handed them over to the Russians.

Tomorrow afternoon I take the blokes on the firing range so it will be late when I get back because the range is sixty-one miles away. There are some good places near this village that we

---

57 Joe was a kitten which Hilda had only had for a short time.
58 In fact, Ronnie did indeed end up going back to his old office job at Robinson's in Rochdale, and continued to work in an office for almost all the rest of his career.

could use for ranges but the trouble is we can't use them because it's all pastureland. Our company went away yesterday on tree felling for the battalion's winter fuel. They have to bring back 10,000 tons of wood by the end of October so they've got a tough job in front of them. It's surprising the amount of timber a battalion uses in a week and you never get half enough. You can't just chop down any tree, you've got to get a permit from the Bürgermeister, and then he marks the tree with chalk to show which ones you can have. All that messing about and everywhere you go in Austria there are trees.

I'm terribly sorry to hear Joe has died. It's awful; there's always something happens to them. I was expecting seeing him when I came home but I suppose it had to be.

The other day a terrible thing happened. A truck took some of the blokes to Graz about thirty-five miles from here. It had been raining rather hard and the truck was returning to camp when it skidded and overturned. Three blokes were killed instantly and six were injured. All the ones killed were only nineteen, had been in the army for seven months, and had just come overseas. What a terrible shock for their parents and what a waste of life it seems. When it's been raining these roads are death traps. The driver of the vehicle was seriously injured. When I'm in a wagon I always see the driver keeps within the speed limit. It wouldn't have happened in this case but the driver was going at forty-five miles an hour. What a terrible thing to happen. It's a warning to the other drivers.

Will you be going to night school again? If so, I'll be able to think of you having your tea Monday nights at the little cafe in Middleton. I'm so glad I used to go to school and meet you because I know what the place is like and I can see you going there.

26.8.46.

As you see by the address, Pop and I finally did get in the Feathers, but we're not sure yet whether they'll have room for us all the time.

We arrived about 4 p.m. and came straight here. It's an interesting old place, half-timbered, oak-panelled walls, wonderful carvings, old pictures, steps everywhere. I go both up and down steps to get to my bedroom. It's very quiet and very posh.

Nothing goes on in Ludlow at night except pubs. I had one drink with Pop in the Feathers' bar tonight. There's a drawing room, a lounge, a reading room, bags of magazines in the lounge, soap and towels provided. Curtains in your bedroom are drawn and bedclothes turned down for you at night.

We had a good journey down. It was typical of Pop and me to set off not knowing which train we were catching or where we should stay, but things worked out for us.

We're going to Birmingham on Wednesday to try and persuade my granny and my cousin Iris to come until Friday and they can stay at my Great-Aunt Jinnie's.

We went along to see her before dinner today. She's about seventy-nine and she's been very ill but she was very glad to see us. It's years since she saw me and she was a bit overwhelmed to see me grown up into such a "smart young lady", such a "cutie". She said I had lovely legs: at seventy-nine she said that! We are a long-lived family you know, and the older they grow the tougher they get, especially the old ladies. I felt sorry for her though, she seems lonely. She has nothing but her cat for company. I wouldn't like to see my parents lonely when they grow old.[59]

Pop is sitting here with me, writing too. We're going out fruit scrumping before we go back. There are apple trees here just groaning with loads of luscious fruit.

How different our surroundings are at present, and yet how close we are to each other. You are in an Austrian village; I'm in a typical English country market town (the first thing we walked into was a cattle market).[60]

It's so quiet here now. The streets are deserted. They are funny, narrow little streets with overhanging houses, mostly half-timbered, hundreds of years old, and even they seem to be sleeping. It's hard to imagine that English and Welsh history has been made within yards of where I'm writing. I must go in the castle again whilst I'm here, and the church too. And I must go through the old gates to Ludford Bridge across the river, climb Whitcliffe Hill behind the castle and think of you. Because you are the lover I once dreamed of.

1.9.46.

I wish I could have been with you in Ludlow, the way you describe the place I could just imagine what it was like. I hope your father enjoyed it, he certainly deserved a holiday.[61]

It was nice of your Aunt Jinnie to say you're a smart young lady. I could see you walking down those English country lanes. I imagined myself walking with you, holding your hand and looking at you.

It's 2 a.m., darling, I'll go to bed now until 6 a.m.

---

59 Very sadly, that is not how things turned out: Edith, Hilda's mother, outlived Wilfred by eighteen years, and she was indeed lonely after he died.

60 The Cattle Market in Ludlow used to be next to the railway station, and the cattle had to be moved regularly down one of the (small) main roads, Corve Street, to get there, past the Feathers Hotel.

61 Because, as always, someone had to be there to look after the shop, as we have seen, Hilda's mother's holiday that summer was a visit to her in Scarborough and her father's was a trip to Ludlow with her.

4.9.46.

11.45 p.m. Wednesday. I was going to write to you last night but I had to go out on another patrol, I didn't get back until 2 o'clock this morning, and then I got up at 6. To crown it all I had to go on another one tonight and got back at 10.30 p.m. I never get a moment to myself.

The reason I've been on so many patrols is because the Russians have been making trouble with the Hungarians. We arrested three Russians and three are now awaiting trial for attempted murder.

By the time you get this letter you'll have started school. You know I'll be thinking about you whatever you do.

28.8.46.

(Written on the Feathers notepaper)

This is the place where we are staying. I couldn't get any postcards yet, so I thought I'd better use their notepaper.

I had a lovely letter from you this morning. I shall always keep your letters. We'll look over our letters to each other some time.

Pop and I have just come back from Birmingham. My granny didn't come back with us because her heart isn't too good but we're trying to persuade her and my cousin Iris, who is twelve and a nice kid, to come over some time to us. We had a mutual showing of photographs and I left her one of you and me taken at Filey.

By the way, the snap I'm enclosing of me watching trains at the age of four was one of my granny's collection. She has lots of them so she said I could have it.

Pop is here now, just up from the bar. We went nutting yesterday and got quite a lot. I also collected several nettle stings and broke my sandal strap. We found two windfall apples on the top of the hedge, and Pop saw a wild pigeon's nest. It was quite nice yesterday but today was blustery and rainy and we didn't miss any good weather by going to Birmingham. Gosh, the local trains are slow. I believe it when they say that God made all creeping things. I'm going to Wellington to see Nancy tomorrow.

Maybe you'll come here with me someday.[62] There's a lovely quiet, well-cared-for atmosphere about the Feathers. That reminds me: I'll put my shoes out to be cleaned tomorrow. Not being used to such comforts I keep forgetting about it.

We went to the local cinema last night. There's no other form of amusement.

418 Halifax Road
Rochdale
Lancs

30.8.46.

Just arrived home and your letter written on the 22nd was waiting for me.

You certainly do seem busy but if I were in the army I'd like a job like that, organising sports and things.

The old chambermaid at the Feathers was sorry to see us go. She said I ought to go there for my honeymoon.

We've brought loads of fruit back with us, but we didn't pick it all. We've got pounds and pounds of pears, apples, nuts, plums. We've got mushrooms too and even a watermelon. We brought my mother some pearl earrings back.

Well, it's back to earth again for me now; no late dinners, no shoes cleaned, no hotel comforts but I'm not really sorry, because it's all very well to live in luxury for a time but I should get tired of it.

---

62 They did indeed go there, and the family tradition of going back to Ludlow has continued to the present day.

And it hasn't been terribly expensive to our surprise. It's worked out at less than £1 a day each and my mother paid £1 at Scarborough for something far inferior to the Feathers.[63]

Pop and I walked round the outside of the castle this morning. We found the seat where I put my initials last time, with my initials on it quite clear. Pop put his initials on. And I also put another "H", so that when I go there with you, I can add a "W".

I was tickled when I heard one porter say to another on Ludlow station today: "That's a nice-looking young lady". I like to look nice for your sake.

1.9.46.

Sunday afternoon. It's raining hard outside, as it has rained for days. We've had no real summer and it's September now. I've got a lot of sunshine to make up for. If we ever go to Australia, I'll get it back then. What do you think your chances are of that job? If you didn't get that one what would you think about going there to get another job? The unknown is always exciting, isn't it? I've always had a longing for adventure. There was something adventurous about the way we got engaged after knowing each other such a short time. We were almost unknown quantities to each other, but I've never regretted it for a second. Acting on impulse isn't always a bad thing.

I'm alone while writing this. Marjorie has gone to see Valerie. My mother has gone to see my cousin Alice[64] *who is in Halifax Infirmary after an operation. Pop is in bed. There is just me, and you in my thoughts.*

---

63 In 2018, the average price per night for a room at the Feathers is £135 without dinner!

64 Alice was Hilda's oldest cousin, born just before the start of the First World War. She and her brother Jack were the children of Edith's eldest brother, Willie Ashworth. He was killed in action aged twenty-six in 1916; his name is on the cenotaph in the centre of Littleborough. Alice had an unhappy marriage, got divorced and never had any children. She was another of the people occasionally called upon to help in the shop.

Don't be surprised but I've actually started knitting. I started last night and I've done 5" already. It's a short-sleeved blue jumper. I'm not very fond of knitting but I have the wool. I've got a bet on with my mother that I'll finish it within a month. I knitted one before and it took months and months.

I'm still not broke, though I have to go to the end of September before payday. Do you know what I bought with the £1 you sent me? I bought some white sandals. It wasn't silly of me to buy them, was it? Something I shall have to get this winter is a coat. I haven't had one for two years and my brown coat is getting too shabby for weekends, but it's all right for school. I think I shall get a utility coat though, so that I shan't have to spend too much money on it. What colour would you like? How about something in tweed? Then it would go with all the other things I have.

I'm having a "stay in" weekend after dashing round the country so much lately. And it's cheap too. All I've spent this weekend is 9d on library fines.

I still have £7.10 shillings left which isn't bad after such an unusually expensive time. I shall have to get Pop up in a minute or two to go to work – first time after his holiday.[65] *He seems ever so much better for it. I think he really enjoyed his taste of luxury in Ludlow.*

6.9.46.

I like the photo, you were a lovely little baby at the age of four. My wallet is bulging with photos now, I love showing them people. It will be wonderful to look back on our letters.

I'm really glad you and your father enjoyed the holiday in Ludlow. What a busy month August had been for you. That seat in Ludlow where you carved your initials, I'll put the "W" there for you when we go together.

---

65   This was Wilfred's night shift in the bakery. The strain of working day and night, as well as being a heavy smoker, eventually took its toll on his health.

I'm glad you're not broke, but if you do ever get short just let me know and I'll send you some money. I only spend about sixteen shillings a week at the most and that goes on cigarettes, tobacco, soap, etc. Sometimes I send my mother a bit of money.

If I don't get that job with Robinson's in Australia I'd still like to go there. As you say, the unknown is always exciting, especially with you.

You did right buying the sandals, I bet they look nice on your lovely feet. Yes, you must get a winter coat, but I really don't know what colour to suggest. You look beautiful in white but it's no use getting that colour for the winter. As you say, something in tweed would go with most of the other things you have.

Since 8 o'clock this morning I've been on the range firing weapons. I fired nearly 2,000 rounds of ammunition, I can't hear a thing! Tomorrow I'm on the range again all day.

3.9.46.

I've been to the pictures at Littleborough with my mother tonight, Rhapsody in Blue.

We have a new kitten. It's just the opposite of Joe. Whereas Joe was sweet, plump and cuddly and playful all the time, this one is a little spitfire – black as night and it doesn't know how to play. I'm going to call it Lucifer because it's a little devil. It spent most of yesterday hiding in the hole underneath the sofa. When we're married, I'd like a kitten and a puppy, wouldn't you?

I've just finished a good book: Bombardier *by Gilbert, a young bombardier's adventures up to the end of Dunkirk.*[66]

---

66   *Bombardier* by Stephen Gilbert, first printed in 1944, was a popular, lightly fictionalised account of the author's own wartime experience. According to the frontispiece of the second impression issued in that year, the book was "produced in complete conformity with the authorized economy standards". In later life Gilbert was better known for his fantasy and horror novels.

9.9.46.

I've been terribly busy this last two days. Saturday morning I went to Radkersburg, a town three miles inside the Hungarian border. It was the trial of six Russians, which took until this morning before it finished. Three of them were tried for killing some Hungarian civilians: their sentence was to be shot tomorrow in Vienna. The other three were tried for attempted murder; they got a life sentence. My job was to keep law and order. It was 11 o'clock both nights before the trials finished.

I'd love to see little Lucifer. I bet she's a little devil, but of course by the time I get home she'll be a big devil. Yes, we must have a cat and a dog when we're married because I like them too.

The book you spoke about, *Bombardier,* I read it ages ago, well, two years ago. I thought it was quite good at the time I read it. I was a bombardier in the artillery, that's corporal in the infantry.

5.9.46.

We've got another kitten besides Lucifer. This one is just about the same age as Lucifer but entirely different. You'll guess how different it is when I tell you I'm going to call it Cuddles. It's really funny to see them together; they're in a state of open war just now. They spit and hiss at each other in turn.

Tonight I've been tidying out a drawer crammed full with papers, diaries, programmes, certificates, exam papers – and all the things that accumulate in the drawer of one who has a mania for not throwing things away, just in case they're likely to be useful someday.

I hate destroying things.[67] *It's unbelievable the varied things there were: diaries from 1937 onwards, old autograph albums, programmes for ballet, opera, plays, concerts. Then there were pencil cases, relics of school days, exam papers which look frightening, music certificates, swimming and life-saving certificates, the hymn sheet from Bill's wedding, typewritten copies of the play we wrote at school and sold for parcels for prisoners. And poems I've written myself.*

You certainly are working hard now, Ronnie. I love hearing about all these things you've been doing — patrols, football matches. Time whizzes past when I'm writing to you yet I don't seem to have said half of what I wanted to say.

11.9.46.

I'd love to see Cuddles, I bet he or she has a tough time with Lucifer but I'm sure they'll soon get used to each other.

Yes, I certainly like sports. I played football again tonight for the battalion against the locals. We won four goals to nil this time. They certainly didn't like the beating; they are horrible sportsmen.

14.9.46.

For a change it's pouring with rain and very cold too. I certainly feel the cold after all the hot weather we've had.

Half an hour ago I was soaking wet. I was out on patrol thirty-five miles from here when the storm came. I was two

---

67 Perhaps fortunately, Hilda did not get very far with the clearing out. She was a tremendous hoarder of documents all her life, and when she died, the diaries and the programmes, college essays and poems were all still there, together with her payslips from the time, receipts for purchases, and all her letters, not just from Ronnie, but from friends as well. Her "mania" in fact provides a fascinating source of information about life at that time.

miles from the nearest house or farmhouse. Other than that there was no shelter at all.

Tomorrow night I take the blokes on a night scheme. It will be about 5 o'clock Monday morning before we finish. The reason for all this training is to get these young blokes really fit so that if any trouble does start, they'll be able to stand up to anything. It's true that an army that isn't fit can't fight.

Last night there was a dance in the village for civilians and squaddies. I was on patrol but I wouldn't have gone in any case because I'm not doing any dancing until I come home and then we'll go together. They supplied far too much drink at the dance last night and I was told this morning nearly everyone there was drunk. They wrecked the dance hall and one civilian was killed, kicked to death. A civvie said this morning some soldier did it. They had an identification parade this morning and two blokes were picked out for the murder. There's going to be a big stink about that. These army dances always end up the same, they go to drink and not to dance. It was the same in Vienna when the Russian officers were killed.

16.9.46.

This will be a short letter as we are having a night scheme tonight. I didn't get back from patrol until 5 o'clock tonight having set out at 7.30 this morning to a village called Ebersdorf on a mountain up in the Austrian Alps. What a climb it was. I was just walking in the clouds which seem to cling to the peaks like cotton wool.

8.9.46.

This is the last day of my holidays. This afternoon I'm going to the bank to put some money in for my mother (and a humble £2 for myself).

I'm glad you weren't in that truck that crashed. I think I should go mad if anything ever happened to you.

I heard this week that demob had been put back two months. Will it affect you? I hope not. If they did put your demob back would you get a leave about Christmas?

We really are going to have a bathroom in. There are going to be all sorts of alterations. Maybe they won't be able to do it all at once because they are only allowed to do £100 of work in one year, but we may be able to get more because of the shop.[68] The surveyor and another chap came on Saturday morning. The bathroom is going to be taken off our room[69] because it is a big room and has two windows. They'll build another wall and alter the doorways. And downstairs we shall have a new fireplace and a kitchen built onto the back of the house, moving the window to the side wall.[70] They'll be doing the bathroom first: it may even be before you come home. The present kitchen will be made into a storeroom for the shop.

How long shall we have for our honeymoon? Shall we be able to afford a fortnight? I still think Cornwall is our best choice. Maybe we could call at Ludlow on our way back.

I'm rather glad you don't want to stay in an office all your life doing more or less the same things day after day. It would be all right for a year or so, but then I think we should want a change.

I'll be meeting the new kids tomorrow. I'm not really sorry to go back to work; time passes more quickly then.

---

68   This is presumably a result of the "Building Restrictions (War-Time Contraventions) Act" passed in 1946.

69   That is, the room shared by Hilda and Marjorie at the time.

70   The bathroom was indeed installed, but the new kitchen never materialised. When the shop was finally sold in 1960, there was still only a tiny scullery acting as a kitchen. The room behind the shop served as a combined lounge and dining room, and also contained the piano. It is where the family spent all their spare time. If the shop was empty, the person serving would go into the back room, and would be alerted that there was a new customer when a bell rang as the shop door was opened.

10.9.46.

I went back to school yesterday. Nothing really outstanding happened. I spent yesterday and most of today giving them tests to grade them 1a or 1b. We have two students from an emergency training college here for three weeks. When they go, two more come and so on, ad infinitum. So we should get an occasional lesson off.

I went to a play with Marjorie last night. Tom had been here all afternoon but when she got home at 11 p.m. he had gone, and she was annoyed. I wish they'd get married. I don't like sleeping with Marjorie.

I can't say how sweet it is of you to offer me money if ever I need it. But honestly, I'd never ask you to send me any. It's not right that I should.

There's only one word for the weather we're having. It's deadly. It rains every day, has done for weeks. I think it's making people despondent.

Have you read about the squatters? I approved of them at first when they just took over old army huts, but now when they're being led like sheep by a set of Communists and taking over private property, I think they're going too far. What do you think?[71]

18.9.46.

Today I've been giving lectures on weapons, field craft, grenades, map reading, compass, etc. Monday, as I told you, I went out on

---

71   By summer 1946 there was a severe housing crisis in Britain. There had been almost no house-building during the war (due to a lack both of materials and of building industry workforce) and many major cities had also seen extensive bomb damage from the Blitz. The squatting arose as a result of this. Also, what was meant to be a temporary measure, "prefabs", i.e. prefabricated concrete bungalows, were built, some of which were constructed at the edge of the small council estate where building started in 1947, and where Hilda and Ronnie would move in 1954. In fact, the prefabs were still there around fifty years later.

a night scheme. The blokes made a real mess of it so they had to do another last night.

The other day out on patrol I heard a wireless. It was playing a waltz. What beautiful memories that brought back to me; I was doing quite well with the waltz, wasn't I?

It hasn't been officially announced whether demob has been put back yet or not but I did hear it had been put back five weeks which would mean I wouldn't get demobbed until the end of January.[72]

I'm so glad you're going to have a bathroom!

You asked me how much demob leave I'll get. I should get about ninety-eight days so that will give us plenty of time to plan and get things ready. Don't worry, I won't be in a hurry to go to work.

You've been grading the kids at school, I've been grading the blokes out here on their knowledge of weapons, etc. Good, fair or bad. Very few of them are good, about sixty per cent fair and the rest bad.

Fancy Marjorie being like that just because Tom didn't wait for her. I know now that their marriage will be a failure because they're not suited to each other.[73] I don't like Tom but I think he'd be different if he had the right girl. Marjorie sticks to him because she is afraid no one else will have her.

It's not fair to your mother and father when they work so hard, they never have the house to themselves. When I have my leave, I shall have more thought for them. Your father is a gentleman and I'll prove to him that I'm the same.

Yes, I've read about the squatters, they've definitely gone too far now. They are going against helping the housing situation. I know they want the houses but they don't grow up out of the ground.

---

72   In fact Ronnie was not demobbed until the end of April.
73   Ronnie was right: the marriage did not last. He was often very perceptive about human nature.

One thing annoys me and that is these blokes returning to civvy street from the forces, they say: "We won the war and this is what we come back to". They seem to forget that the civilians fought a war too. If it wasn't for them England wouldn't be there today. They should be thankful there's an England to return to. You might say England was saved by the RAF, the army and Dunkirk. Maybe, but if the spirit of the people had cracked what good would the army, navy and air force have been?

14.9.46.

Saturday night again and I've had my usual evening: pictures by myself. It was quite a good film, Eric Portman in Wanted for Murder, *the best film of that type I've seen for some time.*

Tom was here all afternoon. Gosh, I'm fed up with them. Never once while you've been away have they offered to take me out for an evening. Don't worry, I'm not feeling sorry for myself and have lots of things to do and everything to look forward to.

I'm thinking of going to some physical recreation classes for women and girls in Rochdale this winter. That will pass one evening on. And then I'll have the modern dance classes on Thursday soon.

We've just got our wireless back at last. We've just heard the news. Now it's The Barretts of Wimpole Street. *It will help me with my knitting if I can listen to something intelligent at the same time.*

It was Friday the 13th yesterday and something certainly happened to me. I had an inspector.[74] We were joking about it at dinner time saying he would come into my class, and he did.

---

74 Hilda had a school friend in Bury who also became a teacher, and between 1947 and the early 1960s wrote and illustrated several humorous books on education, under the pen name Jane Hope. One of these, *The Inspector Suggests*, published in 1951, pokes gentle fun at visits by school inspectors, and gives the advice: "There's nothing to worry about. Inspectors are all right if you know how to handle them...". Hilda seems to have beaten her to it in that approach!

Anyway, my lesson was history. I'd only read the chapter at dinner time in a panic. I hadn't even known what my scheme was until then.

Well, to continue, I read what it was: "Ancient Egypt and Mesopotamia". Can you imagine it? I dashed in and put a map on the board before the kids came in. Then Mr Lowrie, one of the students, asked if he could come and listen to the lesson as he'd been to those places and would like to take a lesson next week. I said yes, and he sat at a back desk sharpening forty pencils for me.

In a few minutes sure enough in came the little man. He saw it was history, then went and sat on another back desk and listened. He said he'd stay about ten minutes but he stayed much longer and then came out to talk to me. He was quite pleasant, didn't criticise at all, and asked all about me, which college, when, etc., then he talked about my courses and several other things and departed in quite a good humour. I'd forgotten all about poor Mr Lowrie. He was still sitting there. He'd sharpened thirty pencils and then broken his razor blade.[75]

But what an experience, to have two people listening, both of whom are very interested in this subject (the inspector was a history specialist) and I who had only just read about it. But I survived, I talked and asked questions, and then let the kids do a sketch map. It wasn't too bad.

The two kittens are lovely now. They go to sleep with their paws around each other and play together and chase each other all over the house. Cuddles is having a good influence on Lucifer.

Do you know what happened this morning, when I could have slept a little longer? At 7.30 Tom went past in a bus and blew his horn loud and long for Marjorie to waken up. The call of a bus driver to his mate! She'd asked him to do it. Isn't it silly?

Pop has some beautiful dahlias in his garden now. We have them in the house every week.

---

75 For lack of pencil sharpeners, it was common to sharpen pencils with a razor blade. In the shop, Wilfred sharpened his with a big knife, which he would then in turn sharpen regularly. The knife still exists.

21.9.46.

At 6 o'clock I play football against the Coldstream Guards. They've come from Trieste. It's just poured with rain today, I got soaking wet and had nowhere to shelter.

Next week all the company will be out for three days and nights on the scheme so I'll take my writing paper with me.

I think of you going to the pictures. I realise how much you miss me when you go on your own, thinking what it was like when we went together.

22.9.46.

10 o'clock Sunday morning and 11 o'clock I've got to go out on patrol. We send out fourteen patrols a day to different parts of Austria, mainly to try and arrest suspected persons and let the Russians see there are plenty of British troops in Austria. Actually there are very few troops now, there is only the 46th division. Before that there was the 48th, 78th and 56th divisions so this division has all their work to do now.

We played the football match last night and drew, one goal each. I didn't enjoy it a bit, pouring with rain, sliding about in the mud, nails sticking in my feet. It was one of those days when everything goes wrong. The last twenty minutes it seemed as though we were playing in the blackout, it went dark all at once and it was only 7 o'clock.

Had a letter from Mother saying she'd asked you to come to tea today so I'll be thinking of you all tonight. I'm glad she asked you, she likes you very much. Mother always says how lovely you are and Hettie too. She says you are a very sensible girl.

By the way, I've got another medal ribbon now, "Services Rendered", a mixture of red, white and blue; that's five altogether.

16.9.46.

Two of our staff were away today. It still makes me mad when I think of my three days' unpaid leave of absence last December[76], and the trouble and backbiting there was. Don't worry, when I want leave of absence to get married, I'll take it.

It's busier at school than it has been for months. I have a large class too, which means lots of books to mark. I reckon I marked well over 1,000 little sums in an hour this morning.

If you went into Hungary for that trial, that's one more country to add to the list of those you've been to. How many countries is that now?

18.9.46.

You'll never guess where I've been tonight. I've been for a Turkish bath with Annie. We thought we'd try it just for once, but we liked it, so we're going again in a fortnight.

I don't know whether you've ever had one. It was quite a novel experience. First, we undressed in a cubicle, then wearing a white cloth that wouldn't have made a sarong for Dorothy Lamour[77], we sat in a very hot room waiting to start sweating. We sat in deckchair contraptions, very comfortable, with a wet towel at the back of the neck and feet in a bowl of warm water. We had to drink cold water to make us sweat more.

Then into the steam room where I really did sweat. After that, laid out on a slab where the attendant gives a hearty scrubbing, rubbing, slapping and rinsing. By this time of course the sarong was discarded.

---

76 In other words, when Hilda and Ronnie first met, and they had such a short time before he had to go back abroad.

77 Famous in particular for the *Road to…* films with Bob Hope and Bing Crosby. She was often depicted in glamorous, exotic surroundings and attire.

Then a long shower, then drying down and, most comfortable of all, to bed for an hour, wrapped in a lovely warm towel and with tea and biscuits. Yes, I'd certainly try it again.

My class is slightly more intelligent than 1b, but there are forty-three of them. Bags of marking![78]

24.9.46.

Yesterday I spent the whole day on the firing range, finished firing at 7.30 p.m. Then I had some tea and checked all the ammunition. The range is forty-three miles from our campsite and it was midnight when I got back.

Today I've been out with maps and compass, etc. looking over the ground ready for this three-day scheme which starts tomorrow morning and finishes 2 a.m. Saturday morning.

This morning I was told that this company and "S" company will be moving to Graz about forty-five miles from here. We're taking over garrison duties there about 10th October, so next week will be the last for this training. I presume it will be much the same as we did in Milan. Trucks are run from this company to Graz every weekend for the purpose of letting the blokes go to the pictures, canteens, etc. I've had the chance to go but never took it because it's a terrible road and takes two hours in the truck. By the time you get there it's time to come back. I hope when we move there, we don't go by civvy train because it takes four and a half hours, it just crawls along. I've been to Graz before, passed through it on my way home. I don't like the place, although it will be better to be in the town for the winter.

You asked me how many countries I've been to: Spain, Gibraltar, North Africa, Egypt, Sicily, Italy, Austria, a little bit of

---

78   It is a tribute to Hilda's skill as a teacher that she never had any trouble controlling such a large class.

Hungary and of course I've been through France and Germany about half a dozen times so I've seen quite a bit of the world.

No, I've never had a Turkish bath: I never need to go to those places to sweat, I do bags of sweating out here every day. I'm glad you and Annie liked it.

26.9.46.

I'm writing this on the scheme. I won't be able to write much because it will be dark in about ten minutes. I'm sitting on an old tree trunk writing this. We're surrounded by forests. Now and again I can hear a bird whistling, otherwise I'm in a wilderness. It's been a beautiful day, I hope it stays like this for the rest of the scheme, though it's very cold at night with the heavy dew. I had no sleep at all last night: at 11 p.m. I went out on a fighting patrol and didn't get back until 7 o'clock this morning, got back just in time for breakfast and off again to attack some enemy positions. I've certainly covered some miles. I started out with eighty-four men. I've got forty-nine left now as the others have been taken prisoner. I thought I'd finished with all this training ages ago, but here I am going stronger than ever. I've got to be thankful it's not the real thing.

28.9.46.

11.30 Saturday night, got back from patrol 10 p.m. I'm dead tired, we finished the scheme at 8 o'clock last night, I was just about on my knees. During the two days we marched forty-nine miles, over hills, through rivers, so you can imagine what it was like. We represented the enemy. In the last eight miles we had to retreat, running like mad all the way. My feet were wet through, and all my clothes, because we swam through a very deep river.

A few blokes couldn't swim so I helped one across. Swimming up the river for 500 yards was certainly hard work, and with full equipment too.

It was freezing out last night, wet everywhere with the dew. I managed to get three hours' sleep and then went out on fighting patrol at 4 o'clock this morning. Three of my men were taken prisoner but we took four of their men (the Hampshire Regiment). At times it was a real mix-up, there were thousands of men everywhere, or so it seemed.

I suppose you've been to the pictures tonight. How I wish I were with you. I can even see your father, Stewart and Edwin playing darts tonight and your mother with Mrs Beresford. I remember when I used to play darts with your father.

21.9.46.

It's Saturday and I'm listening to the wireless. It's the last night of the Proms, and the audience are really enjoying themselves. It's Henry Wood's Fantasia on British Sea Songs. *They've just played the* Sailor's Hornpipe *with the audience clapping out the rhythm and now they are encoring it going quicker and quicker. It's over. Now they're cheering. I'd love to be there.*

I've been to the Regal tonight: Two Sisters from Brooklyn, *fairly good.*

Peggy's husband went to Trieste on Friday night. At any rate, you will be home before he will. I do wish I knew exactly when it will be. I suppose you haven't any idea yet, have you?

I'm going to keep myself awfully busy so that the time will go quickly. I've decided now which classes I'm going to. On Thursday the modern dance starts again. On Tuesday I'm going to classes in Rochdale at Castlemere School. It says it's national ballroom and tap dancing. I'm thinking of joining a class of the Workers' Educational Association, probably the Sunday afternoon class at the art gallery on

"Literature in Society". It starts tomorrow afternoon, so I think I'll go and then go to your mother's afterwards.

I'll let you know what it's like. Speaking of literature, here is the poem you said you'd like me to finish.

To a Lovely Woman
An angel in truth,
A demon in fiction
A woman, the greatest
Of all contradiction.

She'll scream at a cockroach
She's afraid of a mouse,
But she'll tackle a husband
As big as a house.

She'll take him for better,
She'll take him for worse,
She'll split his head open
And then be his nurse.

And then when he's well
And can get out of bed
She'll pick up a kettle
To throw at his head.

She lifts a man up,
She casts a man down.
She makes him her hero;
She makes him her clown.
She's crafty, she's simple,
She's cruel, she's kind.
She's faithful, deceitful,
Keen-sighted and blind.

In the morning she will,
In the evening she won't,
And you're always expecting
She will – but she won't.

There it is, what do you think of it? I think it's quite amusing but not quite true. I don't think I will ever throw kettles at your head and I'm not afraid of mice. I don't think I'm particularly crafty, cruel or deceitful – but then it wasn't written about me.

We had such a time at school yesterday afternoon. It started with a staff meeting about various things. The last item was about dinner duty. Gibby was telling us that we should have to do it regularly, all of us. Wren has never done a dinner duty, and he said he wasn't going to do it. There followed such a row. Wren was abominably rude, and walked out banging the door.

And then, just after the staff meeting, Farrington came rushing down the corridor with a boy who was crying and spurting blood all over the place. It was horrible. He had put his hand through a glass plate and cut his wrist terribly. They took him away in an ambulance. We thought he'd broken it and I don't know about the artery. There was blood all over the hall.

23.9.46.

You're right about the post. I go for days without a letter then get two or three at once. Still, there's nothing we can do, is there?

I like you to tell me all the goings-on in your place, but there do seem to be a lot of murders. You will look after yourself, won't you?

I'll definitely go to those literature lectures at the art gallery on Sunday afternoons. I went yesterday and it seemed quite interesting. We're starting with drama – Marlowe, Chekhov and Shaw – and then going on to poetry from Shakespeare onwards. I've done a lot of this before, but it will refresh my brain before it gets too rusty. School teaching isn't awfully intellectual, and anyway my job has more to do with their bodies than their brains.

I went to your house for tea yesterday and at last I've persuaded your mother and Hettie to come here again a week on Sunday when Pop will be at home.

I think I'm going to go to the Regal tonight with my mother to see Joan Crawford in Mildred Pierce. *I remember it was advertised when we were in London. What memories! I could write a book of them. I say, that's an idea. Maybe I will do some day. I'm sure I could produce an interesting life-story even now.*[79]

I realised that I had forgotten to tell you about the awful weather. It's rained and rained and rained. Floods, railways collapsing, people stranded, roads impassable.

30.9.46.

Came back from patrol 6 o'clock last night and found my watch had been stolen. I made everyone in the company turn his kit out but didn't find it so I've confined everybody to barracks for a fortnight. If it's not returned by that time, I've got the CO's permission to carry on confining. I was raging mad. I made a good start this morning by putting nineteen men on charges; some dirty on parade, filthy rifles, staying in bed after reveille. They all got fourteen days' field punishment. I've just about had enough from these kids just out from Blighty, it's always the same few that spoil it for the good ones. Anyway, they are going to have a very rough time until I get demobbed. I've never felt like this in the army before because I've never had to deal with such rogues.

It's 11 o'clock on Monday night. Today I've been very busy out in the forests chopping trees down ready for our winter fuel. We'll have to get cracking because we haven't half the amount

---

79   Even then, it seems as though Hilda wanted their story to be known.

we need. Then until 10.30 p.m. I was writing out the training programme and wrote four letters to regiments in Austria asking for football fixtures.

I don't suppose Peggy[80] will like her husband going to Trieste, however she can't grumble. Perhaps she would if he'd been abroad as long as I have; three years five months now.

At 7.30 a.m. tomorrow I go out on patrol, this time between the Yugoslav and Hungarian frontiers. We've quite a few miles to cover but we ride about in a truck this time.

25.9.46.

It will be disappointing if demob is officially put back but I guess we'll survive, especially if you get a leave in the meantime. We keep thinking every time: "Surely this is the last time before demob", and it isn't but it's bound to arrive some time.

I keep on telling my mother to get a good supply of bottles in, and I promise whenever you come there'll be some for that occasion. Now we've got some gin and white wine, with a promise of port, and we're still trying.[81]

I honestly don't need any money, but I promise you that if ever I do need any, I'll tell you. Soon I hope I'll have the £3 10s. that the education committee owes me, and it's payday on Monday – and I shan't buy a terribly expensive coat when I decide to get it.

If you really do want to do something it's coupons that are the trouble, so if ever you see any clothes or underclothes to buy, they wouldn't come amiss. If ever you see anything interesting in Austria that we can't get here, either for us or our future home, then it might be a good idea to get that. Just pick up any odd souvenirs that come

---

80 Peggy Jamieson was a friend of Hilda's, another teacher at her school. She was one of the bridesmaids at Hilda and Ronnie's wedding.

81 The shop was also an off-licence, but clearly alcohol was in very short supply.

your way. I mean get something for yourself if you can. Don't think of me.

Being quite practical for a moment, how much money do you think we'll have to start our married life on, buy furniture with, pay for our honeymoon and everything? I think I've about £70 now all told but I hope I'll have a bit more by the time you come. We must reckon up what you need for your clothes when you are demobbed. Sometimes I think that being smart in appearance goes a very long way to being successful. I don't want to start our marriage entirely on the "hire purchase" system or it will be a big drain on our money every week. I still think I can scrounge a bit of furniture from home.

Marjorie and Tom are trying to buy a house now. They have a chance of one. I do hope they'll get it. They'll know tomorrow.

I had a good laugh at school this morning. The kids were putting the feminine of certain words, and one young genius gave the feminine of abbot as Costello. What a mind!

Heard anything more about or from Australia yet?

Do you still have a room to yourself now? How's the weather now? What sort of village is it where you are? How are the civilians? Do you know any German yet?

I'm just listening now to Puccini's opera La Bohème *on the wireless. It's quite a treat to be able to hear some music.*

Gosh, Pop just found a secret passage down in the cellar. He moved one or two loose stones from the wall, and there on the other side is a passage, high enough to walk along, going right under the next house. We couldn't see whether it turned a corner or not. Isn't it thrilling? A real secret passage!

2.10.46.

We move to Graz on 9th October. This company is taking over a prisoner of war camp with 4,000 prisoners and about thirty a day still coming in. They are all Austrian and German criminals, a large number have been tried and are waiting to be shot in the camp. It will be like this time last year when we were at the German POW camp near Milan, on guard every night. It's a great responsibility for the NCOs; there is a court martial if a prisoner escapes. I hate those sorts of jobs but will just have to make the best of it.

I honestly don't know how much money I'll have when I get demobbed. It should be over £100. I hope so anyway because we'll certainly need it.

I haven't heard anything further about Australia yet but I wrote another letter to Robinson's the other day so I'm waiting for a reply.

I still sleep in the same room but I've got a sergeant for company now. He comes from Belfast, not a bad bloke. He's twenty-two, married with one girl. He's only small, was a professional boxer in civvy street. He signed on for twelve years. So far, he's done two years – another ten years, poor devil. It's not very nice for his wife.

28.9.46.

All afternoon I've been sitting out here in the garden writing letters to people I haven't written to for ages. And now after all those words I feel as if I'm not writing this but talking to you.

You say that Pop's a gentleman, and I agree that he is, in all the finest senses of the word. I'm finishing this letter at night now. I decided I didn't want to go out to the pictures again, so instead I'm going to make a good supper for Pop and his pals. We've got a few things to choose from – steak, rabbit, and pressed meat – so I'll make a little menu out for them.

6.10.46.

I was out on training last Thursday and a bloke came to me and told me to pack my kit right away as I had to go to Budapest to the war trials 315 miles away. What a rush it was! They only tried one bloke, an Austrian. He got seventeen years' penal servitude for shooting a New Zealand soldier whilst in a prison camp. Budapest looks very nice or what I saw of it but it's been badly damaged by the Russians. Buda is one town and Pest is the other divided by the river.

I shouldn't have come here[82] until the 10th but I had to take over from a sergeant major in the Royal Artillery who has gone on leave.

My job here is camp sergeant major for administration. What a job. I've got to make out accounts for 711 prisoners, paid out every week. They're allowed ten shillings a week and there are people coming and going every minute of the day. I've written seventeen letters today to other POW camps about transfers, prisoner accounts, replying to letters, as some prisoners state that when they left the camp, they had money in credit and I look up the accounts and find them in debt, so you see everything is in a terrible state due to the bloke who had the job before me not knowing what he was doing.

Since I came here, I've been working until 2 a.m. to try and sort things out but there doesn't appear to be much improvement. I suppose the job will be all right once I get straightened up but heaven knows when that will be.

I'm writing this in my office, looking out of the window. I can see search lights flashing all over the camp, barbed wire all over the place and wooden huts.

Most of the prisoners are in here for war crimes or working for Hitler. There are 105 women in here awaiting

---

82 "Here" is the prisoner of war camp outside Graz Ronnie was expecting to be transferred to.

trial. Some of the prisoners were in the SS, others worked for the Hitler Youth Movement. I believe they are real troublemakers, especially those who worked at the Belsen camp. Three blokes who were in the SS escaped last week so somebody is going to have a rough time watching the prisoners.

I live in a wooden hut with a spring bed. On the whole it's not too bad. I get a prisoner to wash my clothes, clean my boots and bring me water so I can't grumble at that. I give him a couple of cigarettes. A few of the men are allowed out to do jobs in the camp if they are trustworthy. There are some very clever people here, great German musicians, dentists, professors, scientists, poets, or people who worked for the Nazis. Some have been in prison camp since the war ended, some have gone daft with being in too long. There's every nationality under the sun in this camp; Yugoslavs, Poles, Germans, Croats, Romanians, Hungarians, Austrians, Czechs, etc.

Their writing is very hard to read and their names are difficult to pronounce. You just get to know them and they get transferred to another camp and a new lot come in. Some of them are wonderful craftsmen. One bloke has given me a cabinet for my kit. It's very good. Oh, and a lampshade. Some of them speak perfect English, in fact about seven languages. I think that will give you an idea what I'm doing and what the place is like. The camp is about two miles outside Graz.

30.9.46.

October tomorrow and yet another month gone. Time really is moving.

So you're moving to Graz. Well, I do hope you like it and that you will be able to have a bit more free time.

This is a wonderful bit of news, to me at any rate. I've got a dog! Yes, really – and it's lovely. It happened like this. Yesterday morning we noticed a dog hanging around outside the door. It looked like a nice dog, but sort of lost and hungry. Pop said he'd seen it for a few days hanging around, even sleeping in the fields at the back, so we felt sorry for it and gave it some meat and water and so on. It was awfully nervous at first, but gradually plucked up courage and came into the house, and stayed with us all day. I brushed it and we fed it again and it seemed quite happy. We discovered it answered to the name of "Peggy" which suited us down to the ground because I had a dog for years called Peggy.

Well, it slept here last night, played with an old tennis ball, came upstairs to wake me this morning, and generally made itself at home. We were going to report finding it to the police, and then hope that no one would claim it so we could keep it, but today someone told my mother that it belonged to Harrison the farmer. So, feeling very much afraid we were going to lose Peggy, we went to Harrison's tonight to ask them if they'd lost a dog. It was Mrs Harrison who was in, and as soon as we asked her if she'd lost it, she said it was their dog. Then we dropped a hint that we liked the dog, and she said: "If you want it you can have it". She says it's a good dog, there's nothing wrong with it except that it roams. So far, the only roaming it's done is back to our house. It's a lovely dog, a sheepdog, a collie and it's about seven or eight months old, mostly black and white, white paws, chest and long tail. So you see, I've got a companion and protector while you're away, and an intelligent one too. When I finish this letter, I'm going to take Peggy out for a walk. You'll like her, if only we can keep her off the road... [83]

I went to my class again yesterday afternoon and quite enjoyed it. We did Marlowe's Doctor Faustus *which I've done at college so I knew a little bit about it.*

---

83 Peggy was meant to be a working sheepdog (the farmer's sheep were in the field next to Wilfred's hen pen), but according to the farmer she was "too soft" to do the job. She proved to be the most gentle and faithful companion, and lived on well into the 1950s, when one of her jobs became pram guard duty, in the days when people still put their babies outside in the pram, to "get some fresh air".

Yesterday at 4.30 I went to a meeting of Middleton Athletic Association to put in my plea for more equipment. We can't even start to play netball because we haven't got a ball, and there's only one football in the school. I'm getting on quite well with my new kids. Mr Wren is very craftily evading his dinner duties by being absent, which means I have also to play the hymn for assembly in the mornings, and I'm running out of hymns.

3.10.46.

I started a short story this week, and I'll let you know how it goes on. It's a kind of flippant ghost story. I'd like to be able to be a good writer. I don't know why, but I have always liked writing.[84]

I had a very nice letter from your cousin Dorothy[85] in Australia yesterday. It sounds lovely there. They go swimming and surfing every weekend. I'd love that, wouldn't you?

I bet you are tired after that scheme. When are they going to give you a rest? Maybe you'll get one when you go to Graz.

I'm a little bit tired myself today. I've been on playground duty and dinner duty, and then of course it was modern dance tonight. That's one thing I always do enjoy, no matter how tired I am.

Well, Peggy's a great pal. She wakens me up every morning and every night I brush her and take a walk and she loves that.

Last night I went with Annie for another Turkish bath. You don't think we're silly for going, do you? It makes you feel so clean, and it's not expensive, only 2s. 6d.

On Sunday we're having company. Your mother and Hettie are coming, and Annie and Susan, Bill may come, and Auntie Emily too. I do wish you could be here – we'll be thinking of you.

---

84 Hilda's story survived, and is appended to the present book.
85 Dorothy was one of the daughters of Ronnie's Aunt Minnie. She is still alive in 2018.

9.10.46.

It's 1 a.m. Wednesday, just finished working. Since I've come to this camp the earliest I've finished is 11.30 p.m.

This morning I paid 315 prisoners their monthly wages of ten shillings. Today some were transferred to another camp, some went to hospital, some went on release.

The Loyals took over from the Artillery yesterday, and what a mix up there was.

This job is very interesting and no one bothers you except of course there's always someone asking questions, but I'd rather be doing this than guard duty.

I'm so glad you've got a dog. Yes, Peggy will be jealous when I come home, but I hope she realises how lucky she is to have such a beautiful lady to take her for a walk and brush her.

6.10.46.

Your mother and Hettie came to tea today. Your mother will probably tell you about it, but I think they enjoyed themselves. I do hope so anyway. We've been spoiled for choice in food this weekend for once. We had the usual weekend joint – and some steak too. Then we killed a chicken for the occasion. To top all that, someone gave us some meat which we pressed, someone else brought a rabbit, and then a farmer brought us a duck![86]

Peggy was in disgrace this morning. When we came downstairs, she had created absolute chaos. The contents of my handbag were scattered all over the room, a library book had been chewed up, my mother's watch and best hat were on the floor, and Pop's best shoes had a lump chewed out of them. We'll have to get her out of these tricks!

---

86   There was indeed plenty of meat on this occasion, but, as can be seen, mostly not shop-bought.

Marjorie and Tom have decided to buy a house which will be finished by next May, so I suppose they will get married then.

I bought a little 2s. 6d book of Shakespeare's sonnets yesterday when I was doing an errand for my mother in town. So tonight, I'll let Shakespeare say my goodnight for me:
"Then happy I, that love and am beloved
Where I may not remove, or be removed".

11.10.46.

I've just been told to pack my kit, the reason being I'm going to Klagenfurt for some civilian prisoners and will bring them back to this camp.

Klagenfurt is fifty-four miles from Villach towards the Italian border, quite close to the Alps. It's a ten-hour journey from here.

I feel sorry for the NCOs and men because their duties are very heavy with guard for them every other night, and it's terribly cold at night now. I left my shirt hanging on the wall the other night and when I took it down the following morning it had frozen stiff. I wish you could see me every night putting my trousers under the bed. The blokes think I've got an iron because I've always got a good crease in them. I tell these young soldiers[87] it's a matter of personal pride.

13.10.46.

Just got back from Klagenfurt, 10 o'clock Sunday night. I brought fifteen prisoners back with me. On their arrest reports it stated, "A menace to security". Some worked for the German High Command.

---

87   It is easy to forget that Ronnie was still only twenty-two himself!

One of them had lost the use of both his hands which had frozen on the Russian front, and his clothes were dropping off him. It's terrible. One of the blokes spoke perfect English and said he was Hitler's bodyguard. He said Hitler killed himself before the Russians entered Berlin because he'd gone crazy. He said it was terrible in Germany after the Russians occupied it. They raped all the women they could get hold of and VD was all over the place.

Another bloke was a dentist, supposed to be the finest in Austria. There's all sorts of people in this camp.

I feel very tired so I'll finish now and go to bed. By the way, a bloke gave me the enclosed money when I went to Budapest. I think it's valued at 2s.

9.10.46.

I'm sorry you had your watch stolen. It was a dirty trick. I shouldn't like to be in the shoes of the one who did it, if ever you find out.

I was going to write this last night, but after the dancing class my mother insisted on my going to Dearnley with her to a social organised by the Boy Scouts. We had to go out of politeness because my old headmaster bought us the tickets. It was nothing but fourteen-year-old kids or fat old women prancing around in a confined space. The only pleasure of the evening (and a conceited pleasure too) was looking on the Honours Board (it was in my old school[88]) and noticing that nobody had got as many scholarships as me – either before or after. I got three when I was eleven. I'm a conceited little devil, aren't I?[89]

You will be in Graz now, I suppose. Tell me all about it, what the town is like, what your room is like.

---

88   This was the primary school in Dearnley where Hilda's mother, Edith, had also gone as a child.

89   Hilda won a "County Scholarship" to Bury Grammar School in 1935, so her parents never had to pay any school fees.

15.10.46.

What a night I had last night! Some of the military prisoners tried to escape. About 2 o'clock this morning I was awakened by shots all over the camp then somebody dashed in my room and said I was wanted outside. Everybody was running around all over the place, two prisoners had escaped but were recaptured about 6 o'clock this morning hiding in some woods. Luckily no one was hurt. They were two Russians. Most of the prisoners say it's the best camp they've been in and don't want to escape. Anyway, I got back to bed at 5 and was up again at 7. It took me until midnight to reckon some accounts up – I'm going mad with figures.

When I lie in bed and everything is quiet all my thoughts are with you. I imagine what it will be like when we are together. When we are married there will be no boss of the house like there is in so many marriages. It's working and sharing that makes a happy marriage. I realise you know that as well as I do.

Yesterday I got one of the prisoners to put a fireplace in my room. He made a very good job of it. He also made a lamp for my bedside. There's another sergeant in my room now and we're making it quite comfortable. Very shortly we shall have snow and once it starts it will never stop so I'm trying to make the room cosy for the winter.

I don't know how long I will be at this camp but I think it will be until December. I did hear that the battalion may go to Vienna again about the end of the year to do guard duties there. Also, some time next year the battalion may go to Singapore to relieve the First Loyals out there. I enquired again about the release situation. As far as is known, 49 group will be out at the end of January but they are not sure yet.

11.10.46.

I should think it's really an interesting job being with all those prisoners, but of course a very responsible one. Tell me all about them. How is it that they get paid? What do they spend their money on? Do you live in your little wooden hut all by yourself?

Our black kitten has just caught two mice; much growling and spitting! Our animals, we do get some good laughs out of them. Yesterday Peggy went out and came back smelling terrible. I was avoiding her all night, and she would insist on following me. I don't know what she'd been playing in, but it reminded me of the advertisement "Even her best friend wouldn't tell her".[90]

I came back from modern dance last night about 9 o'clock, tired and hungry, and was amazed to find a house full of company. Annie was here, and Mrs Beresford[91] and her boy Brian, and my cousin Alice from Walsden, and, need I say, our two lovebirds[92], as well as Mother and Pop and the animals.

While Lucifer was catching the mouse (first one) in the shop tonight we heard an absolutely terrific crash there. Pop had been on top of the stepladder putting the kitten on a shelf and the steps gave way. Believe me, he wasn't a bit perturbed and the steps are in pieces now. What a man!

Do you ever read horoscopes? No, I guess you haven't the time. Well, mine's next week says I'm going to have a week after my own heart and: "Something you hope for but don't really expect to happen will drop out of the blue". The only thing that could be would be you coming home. I guess it's just wishful thinking.

My week's half-term holiday is the last week in October. I've

---

90 A well-known advertisement for soap at the time.
91 Mrs Beresford was quite a good friend of Hilda's mother's, but it was common then, and for many years afterwards, for women to call their friends Mrs... (and their surname) rather than use their first name.
92 That is, Tom and Marjorie.

heard about a college reunion in Leeds on 2nd November which I'd
like to go to.

13.10.46.

I think a lot about our wedding and how and where we shall live. I
don't know where it will be but I know that even if it's only one room
it will look like a home and I shall make it lovely for you.

We've had another chicken at home today. I suppose we do live
rather well, but my mother has certainly never skimped the food for
us. It's amazing how wonderful parents are when you stop to think,
isn't it?[93]

I shall go to bed early tonight because I just had to drag myself
out of bed this morning. I'll blame it on the alteration in our time —
Greenwich Mean Time now — for the first time in seven years. It's
dark immediately after tea. How does your time compare with ours
now? I can't make out if you're two hours different or the same time.

18.10.46.

We've so much to make up for when I come home, I know we'll
have our whole lives left to do things in. That's the beauty of
meeting each other when we're only young, we've got everything
to live for, everything to be happy about.

You asked me how the prisoners get paid and what they
spend their money on. They get 20 schillings a month (10s.).
That is their own money so they can buy toothpaste, soap,
toothbrushes. If they've no money they go without, but they

---

93   Hilda would certainly not have known at this stage in their relationship,
     because it is not something he liked to talk about, that after the age of
     five, when his father lost his money in the Depression, Ronnie spent
     most of his childhood starving. In fact, materially he was not much
     better off than the prisoners he was writing about.

do get a free soap issue once a month. Men who go out on working parties, with an escort of course, get extra food because it's hard work: coal mines, chopping down trees, and some work on the aerodrome. Some of the women are employed to wash clothes for the prisoners. They also get more food according to my records. There are very few young women in the camp, most of them are forty and over. About a dozen of them were schoolteachers, some of them have babies, but they only come into the camp once a week to see their mothers for about six hours. The prisoners are allowed to write fifty words a week and receive one letter a week. This morning one woman was sent to hospital because she was supposed to be insane. It's not surprising after being in this camp for over a year. Their food consists mostly of thick soup and bread, biscuits twice a week. They get tea and coffee. Some of them whose clothes are worn out are issued with army kit dyed blue.

Some of them are only held temporarily and may be released at any time, others have been here for eighteen months and in other camps too. Heaven knows when they will get out. I'm only thankful I'm not behind these wires myself. I don't think it's right having women in here because none of them is a serious case. A large number of them worked as typists, but just because they worked for Germany they are interned.

I hope you're right about me being home on leave before Christmas. It would be great and there's nothing I want more.

20.10.46.

Once again, I'm going to Klagenfurt, I was going to write to you tonight but I won't be here.

I went out last night for the first time for ages. I went out with a sergeant, Harry. We went to the sergeants' club in Graz, where we played eleven games of table tennis, then went to see

Barbara Stanwick in *The Strange Love of Martha Ivers*.[94] I did enjoy it, it's wonderful to have a bit of time to yourself.

Darling, there is one thing you can do for me, that is, if you go to Manchester any time could you try and get me some medal ribbons? It would be best if you could get a bar with three on and a bar with two ribbons on in this order: 1939-45 Star, North African, Italian ribbon. The other one will be Defence ribbon and the Victory ribbon. That's five: if you have them all on one bar, they stick out too much. Don't go out of your way to get them, we can't get any ribbons at all out here.

16.10.46.

It's been a bit of a hectic day at school today. We've had some gramophone records on order for months. They came today, nine of them, five of which I have already. Isn't that stupid? And to make things a little more ironical the radiogram is broken and I'm having to play the piano myself for dancing. Ah well, I get paid for it so I can't grumble. I reckon I'll save £7 out of this month's salary for my coat and I put £3 10s. in the bank as well.

It's getting quite cold here now so I've actually started wearing a vest this week for the first time for months, but I haven't gone on to stockings yet. Once I start, I shall romp through my coupons.

21.10.46.

I'm writing this from Klagenfurt in the sergeants' mess, transit camp. I didn't arrive here until 9 o'clock this morning because our truck broke down nineteen miles from here stuck in the wilderness. It always happens like that when the truck

---

94   Barbara Stanwick was one of Ronnie's favourite actresses at the time, together with Ingrid Bergman.

breaks down; that was 2 o'clock this morning. It was freezing cold, a good thing I'd got my greatcoat. By the way, one of the prisoners cleaned it for me and made a good job of it, no marks of wet grass now. In one way I feel sorry I've had it done because every time I looked at the marks it reminded me of the glorious time at Filey. I've had the coat five years so it's very thin now.

I must say, you're doing quite well at saving. I don't know how much I've saved because I haven't got my pay book. I'll let you know when I get it back. If I hear of any stockings in Graz, I'll certainly get them for you.

18.10.46.

Ronnie, you'll want a new suit when you come home, won't you? But I've heard that you have to have your name down for months before you can get one made, so I've been wondering if you'd like me to go to Senior's[95] and have your name put down. Shall I do that?

I completely forgot to tell you that I'm not doing night school this time. I've got enough on without it, and in any case, they are wanting the night school jobs for men returning from the services.[96]

Have you heard from Robinson's lately? When you worked there before, what time did you start and finish work? It's a bit silly I suppose to be asking these questions before we have a house but I do like to know little things like that. I think we are agreed that I'll have to go on working because we'll need the money. It's a lot harder for young couples wanting to get married than it used to be.

---

95   Senior's was a men's outfitters shop in Rochdale.
96   People who had had to leave school at a young age, as Ronnie did, to start work, often went to evening classes, known as "night school" to gain qualifications in practical subjects in the hope of getting a better job. Hilda, already a teacher, did not need any additional qualifications, and it was only fair that places on such courses should be left for those who really did need them.

Everything is either on coupons or terribly expensive, but then we knew that things wouldn't be easy-going at first, didn't we?

23.10.46.

I went to the pictures again last night, Joan Crawford in *Mildred Pierce*. I thought it was quite good.

Darling, will you go to Senior's for me and put my name down for a suit?

I haven't heard from Robinson's yet. I wrote to them last week so I'm waiting for a reply. When I worked there, I started at 8.45, 12.30 to 2 was dinner, and I finished at 5.30. So it wasn't so bad.

When I come home and try my luck on the football coupons, who knows I may win a few thousand. I've tried them about half a dozen times and once won £35. It would be okay if I kept that up! Anyway, we'll be much better off than a lot of people, as long as you've got your health, that's everything.

20.10.46.

Last night I went out with my mother for tea up to my auntie's. Spent the evening playing cards for money and lost about 1s. 6d. Bill doesn't half rake in the shekels when he is banker.

Thanks a lot for the note you sent, I'll have quite a collection of this foreign money in a bit.

You are meeting some interesting people amongst your prisoners. Looking at it quite dispassionately, you are having quite an education yourself – University of Life.

Annie was asking me tonight if I would be going to Rochdale Police Ball on December 17th, but I told her not if you weren't home.

I almost forgot to tell you that I made a cake for you this morning, a fruit loaf with nuts on top. I do hope you like it, I made it all myself, getting the recipe in bits and pieces from my mother when she wasn't in the shop.

26.10.46.

Please forgive this paper, I have no notepaper left and had to use this out of the office. Anyway, it's better than none at all.

9 a.m. Saturday morning and at 9.30 I'm going to Trieste taking with me nine German soldiers who are to be tried there for war crimes. It's about twelve hours' journey from here but I'm not staying for the trial.

We had trouble with the prisoners yesterday, they came to me and said they were going on a hunger strike. They said: "We aren't Nazis and shouldn't be in here". I looked on their arrest reports and found they worked for the German High Command. However, we cooled them off by giving them twenty days in the bunker, a cell fifteen-foot underground with no daylight. Bread and water for twenty-eight days should change their minds about hunger strikes.

There are ninety-five people in this camp who have either no legs or arms. A professor is making limbs for them in the camp.

Last night I went to the dentist in this camp. He is supposed to be the finest in Austria. I've no doubt about that; he spent three quarters of an hour on my teeth, cleaning them and filled one of them. The one I had filled at Warminster was only temporary so he refilled it. Before I joined the army, I was really scared of going to the dentist but I think nothing of it now.[97]

---

97 Ronnie used to tell the story that, during the war, new recruits routinely had perfectly good back teeth filled before being sent abroad, because there would be no dentists where they were going, if ever an emergency arose.

Very few Austrians have false teeth, but mostly gold teeth instead. If they have bad teeth the dentist cuts the gum and the nerve so there is no pain.

Saturdays come and go: remember I gave you the ring on Saturday, 1st December 1945? I'll never forget the look on your face, you were so happy.

Fancy you losing 1s. 6d at cards; that's something I've never been interested in. By the way, where did you get the word "shekels" from? You took me back to the old desert days.

It was sweet of you to make a cake, I'll let you know what it's like.

23.10.46.

It's good to think you will probably be home before Christmas even if it isn't demob.

I have almost definitely decided to go to the college reunion now.

Your little hut sounds as if it is getting really homelike with a lamp and a fire. My mother says that if we want to get married before we get a house we could live here, providing that Marjorie has gone, and save a bit of money that way. I want you to tell me honestly what you think of the idea.

Tonight I went to my first (and last) cookery lesson in the Gas Showrooms in Rochdale. After the amount of help we got (nil) I've decided that anybody who can read a recipe can cook. Marjorie and I both made carrot and onion pie and potato cakes. I'm sure everybody in the bus could smell them on the way home.

Speaking of buses, a funny thing happened on the way home from school tonight. The bus had got as far as Heybrook before some bright spark realised we had no conductor on; we'd left him behind. Everybody in the bus was roaring at it. We had to wait until the conductor came along on the next bus.

28.10.46.

Just arrived back from Trieste. On arriving at Trieste with the prisoners I was told to take them to Udine fifty-four miles away from Milan. They should have gone there in the first place: just like the army! It was 3 o'clock this morning when I got to Udine, went to bed at 3.30 and got up at 7. It took us thirteen hours to get back and it was freezing. We had the first fall of snow yesterday which helped to make it a bit warmer. It was much warmer in Italy. As soon as we crossed the border, I could feel the difference.

There aren't many troops in Italy now except Trieste where they still need them.

As soon as I got back tonight, I rang the orderly room and asked them if they'd heard anything about leave. They haven't yet. I just hope to be home for Christmas, which will be my fourth away from home. It's four and a half months since we last saw each other, the longest we've been apart.

You say if we get married before we get a house, we can live with your mother providing Marjorie has gone. Quite frankly I wouldn't like it: one reason is because I'd feel as though I'd always be in the way; two, married families in one home doesn't work out – you can't do exactly what you like. It's very nice indeed of your mother to suggest it. If things were such that we couldn't get a house then I wouldn't mind but probably your mother would think it wasn't her own house.

30.10.46.

As usual, I've only a few minutes in which to write to you. This time I'm going away to play football at the Villach Stadium. I'm playing centre forward for the "Combined Services" against the

Austrians. I was reading the sports section of the forces paper and noticed "Staff Sergeant Williams has been chosen to play for the Combined Services team against the Austrians". I was sure it couldn't be me but I was told a few minutes ago that I was going to Villach at 10 o'clock. It's now 9.40 a.m.

I should get there by 1 o'clock, kick off at 3, finish about 4.45 p.m. and probably get back about 11 p.m. I certainly don't feel like football today, it's pouring with rain. By the time I've finished I'll probably be covered in mud.

By the way, I got my back pay and so far I've saved £33. That's not bad since I came back from leave. If I've enough coupons left, I want to buy you a coat like the white one you've got now.

Prisoners still come and go, even women still come in. Some were school teachers and are forbidden to teach any more. I've got a list of 500 names who are all wanted persons but no trace has been found of them yet. Hundreds are still in civilian jails but gradually they're being sent to these internment camps. In years to come probably all these things will be sorted out.

The truck is waiting for me so I must go now.

26.10.46.

Saturday night again. I went to Annie's for my tea today. I went to take them a rabbit. I went out with Annie and her friend to see a play: Quiet Weekend. *It was a change anyway.*

I told you I was going to have a day out with Annie when I'm going to get my new coat. We've decided to go to Liverpool on Monday because there are some good shops there.

Then next Friday I go to Leeds for the reunion. I've got in at the Mount Hotel with Marion, Jean, Edna and Nancy, but I'm not sure how I'll find it. I've no idea where it is. I had a letter from Mash saying she would meet me at the Queen's Hotel for lunch next Saturday but I've no idea where that is either. The reunion is at the college on Saturday afternoon and evening. Imagine what it will be like when we all meet again: all the talking that will go on, all the showing of photographs and flashing of rings.

I'll have a chance of getting your medal ribbons for you this next week, and I'm really glad to have a chance of getting something for you that you need.

1.11.46.

It's 4 o'clock Friday morning. At 2 o'clock I had to get up again because two more prisoners had escaped, but so far we have not caught them. I took sixty men with me searching for them right to the outskirts of Graz. It's pouring with rain and I got soaking wet but I've just changed my clothes and managed to scrounge a bit of wood.

Everything is so quiet, everybody is asleep, just the rain dripping off the window and the wood crackling in the fire. I like writing to you when it's so quiet.

Yesterday I received your parcel; a million thanks isn't enough. Your cake is terrific. Thanks also for the chewing gum and chocolate; you do think of me. I'm smoking the tobacco now with your pipe and it's very nice. Thank you for being so thoughtful.

By the way, we drew with the Austrians the other day, five goals each, I scored three. Although it was pouring with rain there were 9,000 spectators present, ten minutes from time we were losing five goals to three, then I scored, and five minutes later our right winger scored to make it five all. Three minutes to go we were awarded a penalty, I took it, but was so excited I missed it and it went somewhere in the stands. I could have kicked myself! On the whole it was a good game but very rough. I was just covered in mud plus a gash in my leg from someone's boot.

Enclosed are a five schilling note (value 2s. 6d) and 1s. BAF money which we've just started to use. It's supposed to cut out the black market. They've all got the amount on, 1s., 2s., whatever it is, to be used only in canteens, cinemas, as stated on the voucher. Anyway, you will be able to tell Junior this is what Daddy used when he was a soldier!

I hope you enjoyed the day out with Annie in Liverpool, let me know what your coat is like.

I'll be thinking of you today in Leeds for the reunion. I'm sure you've looked forward to it. Yes, all the showing of photographs and the flashing of rings, I can just imagine it.

I don't know whether I'll be home on December 18th or not. I hope we can go to the police ball but I can't promise anything yet.

Tell Pop I'll try and bring a bottle of whisky home because I might be able to get one in the mess. What a celebration we'll have when I come home. Tell him and his friends I'm looking forward to playing darts with them again, though I'll need bags of practice to catch up with them.

28.10.46.

I've been to Liverpool with Annie today and I've got a new coat.[98] It didn't break me because it's a "utility", but it's a good style; it's got almost a military style about it, simple but smart.

I looked for some medal ribbons but I couldn't get any. I'm going to try to get some tomorrow. My mother is taking me out and I think we may go to Southport. I do seem to be gadding about, don't I?

I bought one or two other things today: some stockings for school, some "Evening in Paris" talcum powder and some chestnuts and walnuts.

---

98   It was quite easy to travel by train. From Smithy Bridge Station a few minutes' walk away from the shop, it was possible to travel directly to Leeds in one direction and Manchester in the other.

30.10.46.

Yesterday I did go to Southport with my mother. It was really a shopping expedition and you know what? It was early closing day! Just like us to choose that day, but we managed to get an hour and a half in before they closed, and that was enough. I got a new dress. It was a "utility" and only £3, and I got it on Lord Street which is supposed to be an ultra-smart, expensive street. It's smart, anyway. It's a deep cherry red woollen dress with three-quarter length sleeves. My mother bought me some lovely earrings with silver fittings at the back.

This seems to be all about clothes so far so I'll talk about food. I had a good laugh at my mother over our lunch. I ordered curried chicken and she, not being quite sure what curried meant, ordered it too. It nearly burned her mouth out.[99]

Then, the shops being closed, we went for a walk. It was a lovely autumn day, sunny and crisp, perfect for the time of year. Like a couple of kids we amused ourselves by a ride on the miniature train. We did laugh at each other sitting so solemnly in this tiny train: the engine had such a silly little whistle.

I like going out with my mother. She says you think I'm always spending but she doesn't do so badly herself. Today she got a new hearthrug and tablecloth and some wine glasses too. And I got two cut-glass wine glasses for our bottom drawer.

I went to Senior's today to see about that suit, and he told me I didn't need to have your name down for January. If you go and see him as soon as you get home, he'll do all he can for you.

---

99 It was very unusual for a restaurant to offer curry in Lancashire in 1946. The first Indian and Chinese restaurants did not open in Rochdale for over twenty years after that, and even then their decor pandered to a popular British style of the time, i.e. flocked wallpaper.

4.11.46.

I'm writing this from a small town just over the Hungarian border. Suddenly yesterday afternoon I had to leave my work, pack a few things and come away on the truck.

I've just a few minutes left and then I'm going back to Graz. I came here for the war trial of two German SS soldiers. Their sentence was to be shot. This afternoon I was escort for the prisoners, tied them to stakes, and out came a firing squad of ten British soldiers. A few seconds later the two men were dead. Just before they were shot, they shouted "Heil Hitler". They died true Nazis. They murdered fifteen people and starved to death thirty-five others in a cell with no light, no clothes, and finally killed them with mustard gas. It wasn't nice seeing them shot but they would have done the same to others if they'd had the chance. If they were set free, they would still do it.

I'm writing this in a very ancient building which was once the school. The beams are hanging down, there are photos of pilgrims on the wall and a statue of Jesus on the cross. I can imagine the school before the war; children's voices, the little desks and I imagine what it would have been like if this had happened to us.

The reason I'm writing in here is because it's next to the court where I've just been. I suppose once upon a time this was a gay little town but now it's dead, heaps of rubbish all over the place. People young and old walk about half dead. What was once a beautiful church is now a graveyard. This is an experience of seeing different things never to be forgotten, an education no one could buy.

I'm longing to see your new dress, deep red cherry, and your pearl earrings.

7.11.46.

I am writing this in the truck going back to Graz. We are now going through the village of Wetzelsdorf thirty-five miles from Graz. I hope you can read this because it's rather hard writing in a truck that's going thirty miles an hour, though it's a smooth road most of the way. With the noise of this wagon and thirty-five prisoners singing in the back it's a wonder I can write at all. These Austrians and Germans are lovely singers.

I've just been back to collect the last of my prisoners. Yesterday I went to fifteen different camps to collect them from Vienna down to Bruck. It was 2 o'clock this morning before I got to bed, got up at 6 and been at it ever since.

Before I left the camp yesterday, I was told the Loyals would be breaking up, as are a number of regiments in Austria, the reason being there are not enough men coming into the army to keep the regiments up to strength. The 2nd Battalion Loyals were supposed to be a regular unit but it's been changed to the 1st Battalion Loyals now, doing garrison duties in Singapore. The changeover or disbanding will take place in the next few weeks, I believe. Where I will go God only knows. It will be a nasty blow for some who have signed up because they want to stay in the Loyals; some will lose their rank, sergeants down to corporal, etc. I won't lose anything because I held the rank of sergeant for over six months, and staff sergeant for five months.

By the way, the CEO spoke to me the other day and said that if I signed on for one year, I would be made sergeant major. This is the second time he's asked me, but my answer was: "Sorry sir, but civvy street is my place with my wife". I don't think he'll ask me again.

1.11.46.

I'm here with Marion in Leeds. I met her at noon in City Square and after much wandering we managed to find this place. We're waiting for Jean and Cynthia to come in now, and Edna and Nancy are coming tomorrow. It's nice meeting the gang again.

Marion and I walked into town today and I tried ever so hard to get those medal ribbons, having failed in Liverpool, Southport and Rochdale, and eventually I found a shop which did sell them, but they told me that the Victory ribbon hasn't been issued to shops in this country yet and told me to tell you to try your quartermaster, but I don't suppose that's much good, is it? However, I'll try later in Manchester.

After our expedition round the shops we had tea and then went to the cinema to see Rex Harrison and Irene Dunne in Anna and the King of Siam. *It was very good.*

To Marion and me, this is just like college. She is sprawling on the bed reading and the only difference is that here the lamps all work and we don't have to change the solitary bulb round from place to place. It seems funny to think that now we're supposed to be grown-up and respectable teachers.

4.11.46.

Well, the reunion is over. I'm glad I went to meet all my old friends. Of course they wanted to know all about you. The hotel was very reasonable: £1 9s. 9d for two full days.

I've got a vague suspicion that Peggy is going to have pups. I've felt a very slight bulge on her.

Things are really moving with regard to the bathroom. They measured the room again today, on Monday it goes before the committee and then they can get started. It's going to cost £145, though it's not supposed to cost more than £100. I do want a bathroom.[100]

I'm glad you spoke out your mind regarding living at home when we're married but don't think I suggested it as a permanent measure. It was only for a temporary home until we get one of our own so that we could get married sooner. I've really thought about my reasons for living here. I'll be methodical:

1. *We could get married sooner.*
2. *We should really have a chance to save to get ourselves some decent things for our own house.*
3. *With us both working we should find it rather pleasant not to do all the housework on coming home from work every day.*
4. *I could turn our bedroom into a wonderful little apartment where we could go and sit when we wanted to and entertain our own friends.*
5. *There would be a bathroom here.*
6. *Mother and Dad wouldn't mind in the least having us here, especially when there's a prospect of us going to Australia some day.*
7. *I think we could live with them without clashing: you'd never feel in the way.*

In spite of all those reasons, I never want us to do anything that would make you unhappy though, or anything that we didn't finally

---

100 The idea of having to go before a committee to get permission to install a bathroom seems extraordinary nowadays. Until they had a bathroom, like most people Hilda and her parents still used a tin bath, and washing was still done in a dolly tub, using a plunger and washboard, with the water subsequently being squeezed out through a manual wringer. In wet weather the washing would then be put on a wooden maiden (clothes horse) to dry in front of the coal fire.

agree on. You see, I don't think houses are going to be plentiful for several months yet. I've been watching the rate at which they build, or rather don't build them. You know Mother and Pop, and you know they wouldn't have offered it to us if they didn't really want to help us out.

I've worked out that it's a year on Friday since I first saw you at Bill's!

10.11.46.

Yesterday I had an afternoon to myself. I went to Graz and was told there were a few pairs of silk stockings in the welfare shop so I dashed away and nearly broke my neck trying to catch a tram. The women in the shop said you are only allowed two pairs but I begged them to let me have more. After a lot of persuading they let me have five pairs of stockings, size 10. I put a duty-free label on then you won't have to pay anything. Let me know when you receive them. After that I went to the pictures to see Charles Laughton in *Captain Kidd*. Not very good. It was on in Rochdale when I was home last.

I'm very glad you enjoyed the reunion. I'm sure you will have lots to talk about. Last time you were together you were girls but now you are women.

Thank you for trying to get the medal ribbons, but don't go out of your way. I've tried the quartermaster but he can't get the ribbon otherwise I wouldn't have asked you.

I know you didn't suggest living in your father's house as a permanent measure but as you say we could get married sooner and turn your bedroom into a wonderful little apartment. I guess that way we wouldn't interfere with your father and mother.

One year on Friday since we first went out together. I felt as though we'd met before: we'd only just got onto Whitworth Road when I said: "Put your arm in mine". Quick work for a man who hadn't been out with a woman before, but something told me, *this is the right girl for you, Ronnie!*

12.11.46.

I'm writing this from Wolfsberg, a small town twenty-five miles north-east of Klagenfurt, where I'm waiting to take some prisoners back to Graz. We spent most of the day trying to find the camp.

Once again please forgive this scruffy paper but I haven't had time to get any. I forgot all about it on Saturday when I went out. By the way, the film *Anna and the King of Siam* is on in Graz this week but I doubt whether I'll get time to see it.

I read in the paper that release groups have slowed up again, because they can't get enough men in the army. I just can't get over it. According to that I won't be out until April. I'll just have to wait and see if that is the case.

6.11.46.

So, I'm engaged to a budding football star! Aren't you glad to be chosen for the Combined Services team? I'm glad for you because I know how much you like football. We really shall go to some matches when you come home. By the way, did you win your match? I expect I'll get to know the result in your next letter.

Tom has been almost living here this week because Marjorie is at home. He even had his dinner here yesterday (and tea and supper). They are going to Blackpool to his sister's this weekend.

There was a big bonfire in Smallbridge last night but I couldn't go because it was one of my dancing classes.

It is sweet of you to say you'll buy me a white coat when you come home. You know that's just what I want. I think it's marvellous

that you saved £33. We're going to get you some lovely clothes though
before we spend any money on me.

14.11.46.

I've just arrived back from a small village fifteen miles over the
Czechoslovakian border, as usual to collect more prisoners. We
are dragging them in now, three blokes, they are accused of
being war criminals and the war finished over a year ago.

We left at 5 o'clock last night but didn't get here until 2
o'clock this morning. The wagon got stuck in the snow up on the
mountains, eighteen miles of nothing but winding roads right
up in the sky. It was beautiful but terribly cold. I slept in a barn
(we brought our own beds with us) but it was lovely and warm.
I saw the Bürgermeister about the prisoners. He couldn't speak
English; you should have heard me mixing what little German
I know with Italian and English. Anyway, he must have guessed
what I wanted.

When I opened the door of my room as we got back, I
noticed there was a letter from you on the table. Was I glad to
see it.

Yes, I won't forget the white coat, long or short whichever
you want, even to my last penny I'll buy it.

8.11.46.

Today is our first anniversary. The first time I saw you I shall never
forget it. You were sitting there at Bill's when I came down from
my bath. Just think, if I'd been half an hour longer in the bath, I
might have missed you altogether. What slender chances our lives
are based on. I wonder what we'll be doing next year on our second
anniversary of meeting each other?

Gosh, but it's cold here now. A biting North-Easter blew the fog away, and now it's nearly blowing us away.

It's now about four months since I last saw you and every day seems like a year. It's Armistice Day Monday. I shall be thinking of you in the silence, and thanking God that you are safe.

10.11.46.

I went to the Regal with my mother last night, Tyrone Power in Jesse James, *not exactly her type of film, but it wasn't too bad. Have you managed to get out any more often lately?*

Peggy has developed a squint. It's just come on in these last few days and the peculiar thing is that her eyes are turning out. I've never seen a cross-eyed dog, let alone a dog that squints sideways. What can I do about it? She is all right in every other way, quite healthy, and her coat's in beautiful condition.

I've got one address in Cornwall if ever we want to go on our honeymoon there. I got it from Mr Rothwell who is the recently retired electrical engineer from Birch Hill.[101] He called here yesterday and he is a wonderful pianist. Every time he came in the shop, he used to stay to play the piano for a few minutes. Then he said he might be going to Cornwall in the spring so I asked him if he knew any addresses and he gave me one. So that's one place we can put on our list. What do you think about it?

16.11.46.

Once again, I'm playing football this afternoon in the Vienna Stadium. It's now 9 o'clock and I'm leaving here at 9.20 which doesn't leave me much time because we kick off at 2.30 this afternoon. I didn't know until this morning because last night

---

101 The local hospital on the way to Littleborough.

I was collecting some prisoners and didn't get back to camp until 3 o'clock this morning. At 7 o'clock a bloke woke me up and said: "You're playing football in Vienna today for the BTA team". I was certainly surprised because out of the eleven men in the BTA team nine of them are professionals. We are playing the all-Austrian eleven so it should be a good game. It's an ideal day for football, cool and the sun shining. I suppose I'll come back tomorrow unless there's a train tonight. I'm playing centre forward again – I'm hoping there's no penalty kicks to take this time. I read the forces paper this morning and it said: "Staff Sergeant Williams 2nd Loyals put up a grand display as centre forward for the Combined Services so is chosen to play for the BTA 11 in Vienna today". Anyway, I'll give you my summary of the match in my next letter.

I called in the orderly room yesterday and the clerk told me I should be going on leave in about a fortnight at the latest. I've got my fingers crossed. If I get leave in a fortnight it will mean I may get Christmas at home but if my leave expires a few days before I wouldn't go back. It would be my first Christmas at home in five years.

I'm glad you got that address in Cornwall, it may be very useful. I've been to Cornwall, there used to be a Royal Artillery firing camp there. I went with the artillery for three weeks in summer 1942.

18.11.46.

I'm writing this on the train from Vienna. There was no train last night so I had to wait until 8 o'clock this morning. It's rather awkward writing on these trains, shaking all over the place. There should have been a train last night. I waited for hours and finally I was told that the train had derailed seven miles from Budapest, so at 3 o'clock this morning I dragged myself back to the hotel where I went after the match. Wasn't it lucky I wasn't on that train!

I went to the pictures in Vienna and saw *Anna and the King of Siam*. Yes, it was very good indeed. I thought Rex Harrison was outstanding. It seems strange walking through the streets of Vienna on my own. I don't enjoy going to the pictures on my own either.

Well, we won our match with the Austrians by one goal to nil. It was a great game. There were 24,000 spectators, about half of them British troops and the rest Austrians. Talk about the crowd roar; they nearly sent me daft. The game stopped for ten minutes because some of our troops were fighting with the Austrians. It all started when we should have been awarded a penalty, but the referee, being a German, didn't want to see it. Our inside right scored the only goal of the match in the last minute. What a great goal it was. He hit the ball with such force from the edge of the penalty area that it split the net and the goalkeeper was lying on the floor helpless. That's when the crowd really roared.

12.11.46.

It's a pity you missed that penalty and didn't win the match, but all the same I think you did awfully well to score three goals yourself.

Good news: the licence for our bathroom and new fireplace[102] has come through and they're actually starting work the day after tomorrow. It will probably be a state of chaos here for the next few weeks, but it's going to be worth it.

---

102 The decision to have a new upstairs bathroom and downstairs fireplace may seem like an odd combination, but in fact the coal fire was essential for the bathroom. A back boiler was installed in the wall above the fire, and this provided the hot water. Central heating was never installed: even when Wilfred and Edith retired in 1960 and had a new bungalow built, their hot water supply was obtained from a Baxi back boiler above the fire.

It was gruesome for you to have to watch those men being shot. The sights you've seen! Don't ever let them make you hard inside. I suppose sights like that and war in general are bound to have a profound effect on men. I think that with you it's just served to toughen you, whereas a weaker character might have been warped for life. I guess it's been like that with a lot of people. Their minds and feelings have got hurt by what they've seen and experienced, and things like that take a long time to heal. I think that is one of the worst and most terrible effects of war – its effects on people mentally, morally and spiritually, even more so than physically.

I'm so glad you like the cake. I love doing things for you. I bet you've used all the chewing gum up already!

I read in the paper today that Group 46 is being demobbed December 25th to January 31st. If that's true, when will Group 49 come out? Is it still only one group a month? Surely they will give you leave if your release is to be so late. Isn't it maddening? This Labour Government which promised such great things hasn't kept any of its wonderful promises. "Get the men home", they said. Look how things are now. Their great recruiting campaign was one big flop. The amount of interference and control and hindrance there is in private lives these days is absolutely maddening.

14.11.46.

This afternoon we took some of the kids down to a concert in Middleton. It was an awful concert. The idea of taking them to hear music was good but the type of music was completely batty. It was a string quartet. Chamber music of all things! If it had been a full orchestra, playing some light, popular classics, it would have been good, but for the education committee to choose a string quartet shows how little they know children. I felt sorry for the kids. In the interval they told me how bored they were.

Yesterday teatime my mother and I went to choose a new fireplace. We're not quite sure which one we'll have yet but both are nice.

Last night I was moving furniture upstairs. We found all sorts of things when we cleared out some boxes and drawers in my mother's room, things we haven't seen for years. I was thrilled when we found my old dolls. There was Brenda, a baby doll —one arm, wearing some pale pink woollen panties I once knitted her when I was a little girl. There was Teddy, my big cuddly bear that Pop once bought for me in Blackpool, slightly moth-eaten and disabled but nevertheless, my teddy. And my favourite doll of all, a big one, just like a live baby, called Willie. I called him that after Bill. I used to think he was wonderful. I shall never forget the Christmas morning I went downstairs, and there was Willie, complete with pram. A child's dream of heaven[103]

We found my grandmother's brooches, and even my great-grandfather's burial certificate – 1868 in St John's churchyard. I guess when we've been married a few years we'll have a unique collection of old junk that I put away in case it comes in handy. You'll have to be very neat and tidy to compensate for me. I'm warning you, I'm simply not methodical by nature. One thing though, I do like things to be clean and comfortable.

19.11.46.

Today is the first day for over a week that I've been able to do any work in my office. Someone had done a bit for me but you should have seen the pile of accounts there was. I started on them at 8 o'clock this morning and was still at it at 10 o'clock tonight.

Don't worry, the sights I've seen will never make me hard inside. In fact they make me feel just the opposite. I'm thankful to

---

103 Willie was destined to survive long enough for another two generations to play with him.

have come through safe, and appreciate what health and freedom is. Yes, the army certainly made a man of me. I was just eighteen when I was called up and the army has toughened me in many ways, taught me to look after myself, speak up for myself. There is no comradeship so great as that in the army. Not so much now, because the war is over and these young kids haven't learnt the meaning of it yet. Millions of good men have been killed, but it's when you have been through hardship you really value your life. Before I joined the army, I didn't appreciate a lot of things, the things Mother did for me and the way she'd always looked after me. I took a lot for granted, but I've missed those things deeply.

Yes, this Labour Government made a grave mistake promising so many things. No wonder they get no volunteers for the forces the way things are going. They talk about fighting for your country but don't know what it means. It's just the same as after the last war; thousands of poor devils forgotten, and what thanks did they get?

I'm longing to see the new fireplace, it will make all the difference to the home.

21.11.46.

Once again I'm writing this in a truck going to Feldbach, a town twenty-five miles north-east of Graz where there are five more prisoners to collect from the civilian jail.

Yesterday I didn't get a second to myself; 2 o'clock this morning when I got to bed. I went to Trieste again to collect more prisoners, running round Trieste all day picking them up in different places.

Well, I'm expecting to know whether I'll be coming home on leave or not this weekend. If I am I'll be writing it in great big block letters because I'll be too excited to do anything else. It will be nineteen days of heaven.

In less than a fortnight the West Yorkshire Regiment will have taken over the prison camp ready for the Loyals breaking up, so I want to get my leave before then, otherwise I might have to wait ages or get none at all.

17.11.46.

If only you could get leave before Christmas. If you could I should probably be at home most of the time. You see we had a pleasant surprise on Friday morning at school. The big boiler burst. We had to close school because it's so cold and there was no heating, and it may be a few weeks before the new boiler arrives and is put in. When DB told the kids they all cheered. We're not completely on holiday because we have to go in on our duty day (Thursday is mine) to supervise dinner duty and any kids who might be there to play in the playground but that's not work.

In any case, it's a good job the boiler did burst, because yesterday Manchester bus workers went on strike because of one of their drivers being sacked, and the 17 route is stopped completely, also the 59 route. Rochdale buses are only going as far as the boundary, so if I had to get to school tomorrow I should have an awfully long walk. They might not even be running by Thursday.

If the boiler isn't in soon I shall have to take my turn in doing a few days at another school as a supply teacher.

I went to Littleborough pictures with my mother last night. We started by going to Rochdale but every place was booked up and at the Regal there was a terrific queue, so we went straight on to Littleborough and saw Johnny Angel *at the Queen's. Today I've been to the chapel with my auntie and uncle and Mother. I think you'd like to be married in church, wouldn't you?[104]*

---

104 Ronnie had been baptised and confirmed in the Church of England, but Hilda, like her mother, had been brought up as a Methodist in Dearnley. Her Great Uncle Stephen was a Methodist minister, and she was baptised in water that he had brought back from the River Jordan in the 1920s.

One of our cock chickens was run over last week. Both legs were smashed, so Pop had to kill it and we ate it today. It was one of those we were saving until Christmas too.

It's Monday morning now, and the bus strike has spread all over Manchester; no buses, trams; nothing!

19.11.46.

Two of your letters came yesterday. I see that you've heard about the demob slow-up; isn't it dreadful? But surely there will be leave for you now.

The bus strike has got worse. All the bus depots in Manchester are on strike now, and tomorrow some from surrounding districts will be coming out. I have no sympathy whatsoever for the strikers. They seem to forget just one important thing, that their job is to give service to the public. If I'd had to go to school every day this week I would be in a sorry state. On Thursday I think I'll go on the special bus that Rochdale runs to Middleton Grammar School.

The news is on now, and it seems to be strikes, strikes, strikes, and rationing.

It's just been announced that 1,700 more Cheshire bus workers have come out on strike as a protest against Manchester using volunteers to drive buses. The poor volunteers were stoned by pickets anyway. It makes my blood boil to think that grown men can behave in such childish ways.

I was looking at the stars last night just outside the house. I can't ever remember seeing them lovelier. It makes me happy to think that you can see the same stars. There was Orion in all its winter glory, Pegasus, Cassiopeia, the Northern Cross, and they looked so beautiful. Then suddenly, I saw two shooting stars: they flew down as clearly as anything, and I made two wishes. I mustn't tell you what they were, but you'll guess right first time.

When you see the stars, think to yourself that I, at the same moment, may be looking at the same stars, and maybe even wishing on a shooting star for the things we both want.

You seem to lead a very wandering sort of existence at present, chasing round after all these prisoners in places with unpronounceable names. It doesn't matter what sort of paper you write on, your letters are still you.

Mother and Dad have gone out together tonight. It's the first time for ages that they've had the chance. They've gone to a whist drive and dance organised by the Off-licence Association. They were looking forward to it.

The men haven't started on our bathroom yet because the weather has held them up, but they'll be starting soon. We've got our licence, cost of work not to exceed £93. It's a bit thick with all this housing shortage when we can't have existing houses made as comfortable and habitable as possible. I'm afraid the things we want doing come to more than £93, but every single thing is a necessity and not a luxury.

We've got some chestnuts to sell in the shop now – great big fat ones. I love chestnuts. My idea of heaven would be to sit here with you in front of a roaring fire for the evening, eating roasted chestnuts.

23.11.46.

DARLING, I'M COMING HOME! I'm too excited to say anything, my brain is in a terrific whirl, my heart is beating madly. God was with us, I knew it would come true. I leave the camp Friday 29th November and should be home about the 3rd or 4th December. My pen won't go fast enough for the things I want to say.

I hope the bus strikes aren't on when I come home but it wouldn't make any difference because it wouldn't stop me from getting home. I've certainly no time for these men going out on strike.

Yes, I often look at the stars and think Hilda can see the same stars. Very soon now we'll be seeing them together. Believe me, it doesn't matter if there's no fireplace in when I come home, as long as I'm with you that's all that matters.

The sergeants and officers have arranged a party for me because they may not see me again. One of the officers cried; he must think something about me.

Some of Hilda's letters up to the end of November were redirected to England: Ronnie clearly did not receive them before he went on leave. Hilda had already written to him several times before she received the letter telling that he would be coming home.

22.11.46.

I've just got your letter telling me about the five pairs of stockings. I can't thank you enough! Conscience bites me a little. Do you think Hettie needs some stockings? It mustn't be such a good thing for a girl when her brother gets engaged because the fiancée comes in for so much of his attention. Don't you think when you come home again that we could persuade her to come out with us for an evening?[105] I seem to see so little of her and your mother.

I went to school yesterday for my duty day (the bus strike having ended the previous evening) but there wasn't any work to do. Next week I have to go as a supply teacher to Rhodes. It may take months before the new boiler is in at our school. They're not likely to pay us money for doing nothing so they may send us out as semi-permanent supplies to other schools.

---

105 Hettie had no social skills, and sadly, no friends. She could do her own shopping, and occasionally she would go to the cinema on her own. She could read and write, but her reading matter consisted of children's comics which she bought from a stall on the market.

Do you know where Rhodes is? It's between Middleton and Manchester. The headmaster is Mr Ashworth, my former night school boss. I don't know anybody else who is there. I believe I may have to take quite a young junior class. That will be a change after two years of seniors. It's a queer position to be in, but at least I've had a week off.

Those men haven't been to start in our bathroom yet because the surveyor had drawn the plans without a lavatory in, saying that we should go above our licence if we had one. But my mother's talked him round and he's making more plans so that we can have one. Do you know what he said? "Young lady, I've got a date with you; when you have your first bath in your new bathroom I'm going to come round and scrub your back".[106]

24.11.46.

Now that I know your demob is slowed up I keep on hoping that your leave will be just at the right time that will allow you to be home for Christmas. It would be lovely for us to spend Christmas together.

I go to Rhodes tomorrow for a week as a supply teacher. I don't even know how to find the school but I guess I'll arrive some time. I'll let you know what it's like. Peggy's eyes have gone back to normal! She's showing her sheepdog instincts by herding the kittens in whenever they go outside, even picking them up in her mouth. She even rounds the hens up when it's feeding time.

26.11.46.

I've got four of your letters to reply to! I knew the post was wrong and that there were some more on the way.

---

106 It was not an era of political correctness!

This class I've got at Rhodes is a class of seven-year-olds. I don't like the school as much as ours, neither the building nor the staff.

I'm so proud of you and your football. I bet you played well in your match in Vienna. You must be good or they wouldn't keep choosing you. It shows you must be as good as these professionals.

I had a letter from your mother asking me to tea a week on Sunday. How lovely it would be if you were there. It's a year on Saturday since the day we got engaged. My happiest year!

28.11.46.

I've had a day at home today. Yesterday at school I suddenly developed a beauty of a cold. So I've had a day in bed.

I've been thinking of all the things we could do if you're home for Christmas. I wonder if we could get in at a Manchester pantomime? And would you like to help me with my Christmas shopping? I haven't bought a thing yet, waiting for payday.

Peggy has been a little love today. She's been upstairs to look at me dozens of times. My mother even sent her up with the paper this morning. It's nice to be spoiled for a day occasionally, isn't it? We're departing from our Thursday routine of pie and peas and having boiled onions for our supper tonight because my mother is a firm believer in boiled onions as a cold cure.

30.11.46.

I'm hoping that you'll be on leave before this letter arrives in Austria, and I shall have seen you before you read it. If only I could! But just supposing your leave didn't come off yet, I couldn't bear to think of you out there waiting for letters, so whatever happens I'm writing. This suspense is terrible. I do believe my mother is wanting you to get your leave almost as much as I am. She keeps consoling me with the thought that you may be home soon. I feel much better now than the last time I wrote. What other news is there? Lucifer stole a piece of fish yesterday. Cuddles *climbed a tree and did a Tarzan act from a branch when a bird flew overhead and startled her. Afterwards she got herself upside down. We laughed until we cried. The weather is still dreadful. I'm reading* Vanity Fair *for the third time. I went to the pictures again by myself tonight and saw Walt Disney's* Make Mine Music *at the Regal. And that's all the news I have.*[107]

---

107 Hilda has obviously not yet received Ronnie's letter of 23rd November at this point.

There are no letters from December 1946 because Ronnie finally did come home on leave. After his leave, Ronnie was sent back to Austria for a month, but never really settled down again. It was clear that there was no longer as much for him to do, and because it was not certain where and when he would next be moved, he could not give Hilda an address to write to him, although he could still write to her, which he did. In that month, nevertheless, Hilda wrote a total of seventeen letters which she was unable to post, and she gave them to Ronnie when he next came home. So in that time she knew what he was doing, but he had no idea what she was doing.

30.12.46 Letter 1

Last night at this time you were here with me by the fire. Tonight you are hundreds of miles away, and I miss you terribly. Look after yourself, I do hope that everything will be all right for you.

I shan't write a long letter now as I have to be up fairly early in the morning. I have my packing to do and I'm catching the 12.30 train in Manchester.[108] I'll be thinking of you travelling.

Thank you for those unforgettable weeks. I shall always treasure them.

---

108 Hilda was going to visit Marion, one of her college friends who lived near Scunthorpe.

30.12.46.

I didn't arrive at Euston until 9.20, five and a quarter hours from Manchester, mostly due to the fog. I fell asleep for two hours on the train, and the rest of the time just sat quietly and thought of you and the glorious leave I spent with you.

I'm writing this sitting on my bed in the Salvation Army, five minutes' walk from Euston Station. It's only 1s. 3d for bed and breakfast.

I hope your mother enjoyed the film and I thought of you both.

I'm not writing a long letter because my heart is too full for words. I'll try to write tomorrow at Calais. I hope you enjoy yourself with Marion, I'll be thinking of you, as always.

Remember me to your mother and father and thank them for me for being so nice to me.

31.1.47   Letter 2

I've got about half an hour to wait, one sheet of notepaper and some ink in my pen and I must write to you. I've been thinking of you. Now you'll probably be in Dover waiting for a boat. I was thinking this morning just before 10 that you'd be showing your pass and keeping my fingers crossed that everything would be all right.

There are no words for how I felt this morning waking up and knowing that I should not be seeing you today. I suppose I ought to be, and I am, thankful for having you for a month, but I shall never be satisfied until you are home for good.

Little do the other people in this waiting room know that the girl writing in the corner is pouring out all the love in the world to her beloved. Romance on the railway station! There's romance everywhere if only people knew where to look for it. I'm so glad we found it together. I get tears inside me when I think of you going back on that awful journey. I shall be thinking of you especially at midnight tonight, hoping to make our wishes for the New Year come true.

31.12.46.

I'm writing this sitting on my bed in Calais transit camp, it's 11.10 p.m. I've been messing about at Dover and getting blankets, signing papers, had a meal, wash and shave. It's surprising how long it takes when there are a few hundred troops.

Forgive the writing as I can just about see to write this. There is one bulb in this large Nissen hut. I don't think we are leaving here until 6.30 tomorrow night, the reason being there isn't enough fuel for the trains so I won't get to Villach until sometime Friday night.

I got through with the pass all right, thank God. I altered the number on the station from 273 to 283; in other words I just changed 7 into 8. It looked perfect. It was worth it.[109]

I realise how lucky I was getting the leave. I enjoyed every moment of it with you. I admit I looked very serious sometimes, but I was thinking how wonderful it was to be with you.

A very, very happy New Year, I know it will be happy for both of us because it won't be very long before we'll be together forever.

---

109 Once again, Ronnie has altered the return date of his leave, but this time by ten days! If he had returned on the date he was supposed to, he would have missed Christmas at home yet again. It is very difficult to blame him, but he was taking an enormous risk. In later years he spoke about his fear. Since his regiment was being disbanded in any case though, one wonders how much it really mattered.

1.1.47.

I'm writing this from Calais at 4 p.m. I'll be glad when I know where I'm going.

I feel much happier to know it's my last time away from you and it shouldn't be very long either. I'll write again from Villach.

Crowle

Lincs

2.1.47   Letter 3

I wonder where you will be by the time you receive these letters. At any rate, the worst part of your journey will be over now. I only hope that you don't have to stay in Villach too long.

I arrived a little bit sooner than expected. I'd booked to Scunthorpe, but when I arrived at Doncaster I found that Crowle was before Scunthorpe, and as I'd wired Marion to meet me at Scunthorpe I had to do a bit of quick thinking. I rang from Doncaster (having an argument with the telephone operator when my penny got stuck in the slot, and she was too dumb to understand) and Marion met me at Crowle.

It's very countrified here. Marion lives in quite a big house, and her young brother and sister are home from school. We spent New Year's Eve very quietly, going to the only cinema to see State Fair, *which we'd both seen before, then sitting listening to the wireless until just after midnight. I did think of you.*

Then yesterday, we cycled a few miles to The Grange, a farm where relations of hers live.

162

Later we played table tennis, and we had a goose for dinner.

Today we're going into Scunthorpe to the cinema, buses permitting, because there are only three a day.

So you see I'm leading the simple life.

418 Halifax Road

Rochdale

Lancs

4.1.47　Letter 4

I got two of your letters this morning, written from Calais. I'm so glad you got through all right in London. You really deserve to anyway. It's a crying shame that you and others like you are still in the army. If only they would decide to send you back to England.

I can't believe it's only a week since you were here playing draughts with me, and I was sniffing and sneezing all over you.

I had quite a good journey home yesterday. I had my lunch in the dining car on the train, the first time I've done that since before the war.

Now you will be in Villach. I followed all the stages of your journey in my imagination. Pop is sitting down doing the books as I'm writing this. He says he hopes you are not too bored. I gave him all your messages and he seemed pleased with them.

They've actually started on our bathroom this morning. The first week, it appears that they are going to be engaged in putting pipes in.

I was out for an hour or two with my mother this teatime. She bought a new hat and then we went to the Carlton for our tea. It did seem funny going there without you. They've taken the Christmas tree away now.

After tea I went to the Empire by myself. It was George Raft in Mr Ace. *I could hardly believe that it was in the same cinema the week before that I saw the trailer for that film.*

Before I started this letter I was helping Pop to write an appeal against the Income Tax assessment of my mother's profits. Their assessment is ridiculous. It says her profits are £600 a year.[110] Why, if that was true, none of us others would need to work. So we certainly are appealing, and getting our dim auditors to help if they can.

4.1.47.

I'm writing this from Villach; arrived here at 11 o'clock last night. It won't be a long letter because my hands are so cold. It's freezing everywhere in this camp. Remember the Sunday we started out for a walk and it was so cold we turned back? Well, it's as cold as that, snowing, feet deep in most parts and like glass underfoot.

As I told you in my last letter we were leaving Calais on the 6.30 p.m. train. We got on the train at 6 p.m. but there was no engine and one didn't arrive until 11 p.m. There were no lights on the train and we just sat in the dark for five hours doing nothing. We didn't get a drink or a meal until 1 p.m. the following day, nineteen hours without! It's a good thing I had your sweets and chewing gum.

I don't know when I'll leave this camp. They've told me the Loyals haven't quite finished breaking up. I'll be going to Graz but where I'll finish up I don't know. As soon as I get an address I'll let you know.

Most of the Loyal sergeants and NCOs left this camp this morning; some were going to Italy, Palestine and Germany. They all had a year or so to do in the army. They were surprised to see me; didn't expect me back.

---

110 The shop was a good, solid business, and the family had many loyal customers. But they would never be rich, and £600 profit was clearly an absurd amount to pay tax on in 1946.

5.1.47.

I left Villach 9 o'clock Saturday night (last night). It's normally a six-hour journey but it took fourteen hours.

I'm writing this in Graz at the Loyals' headquarters. I suppose you'll just be going to bed after spending the afternoon with Mother and Hettie.

I still can't give you any address. There are only about twenty of us left. I believe the last of the postings finish on 10th January so I should know by then where I'm going and what my address will be. It's bad enough coming back to a unit from leave any time, but to hang about like this is awful.

It's freezing, I've honestly never known it to be so cold in all my life. What with the snow and ice it's 19° below freezing point. I'm just aching with cold feet and hands. I put Vaseline on my hands and face to stop the pain. There is no water in the billets, no fires, and only two blankets to sleep with. I'm using my gas cape, greatcoat, or anything to keep me warm. It's a wonder I can write this letter. I had to go into Graz to have a wash and shave this afternoon.

There's a great ice-skating competition in Graz with competitors from all parts of the world. It's held this time every year on an open-air arena. I believe it's wonderful but anyone who goes will die with the cold.

There's a hospital near these billets so I'm going there tomorrow for a bath: I certainly feel like one after all that travelling.

Don't worry that you can't send your letters on yet, as long as you are getting mine that's all I want because I know you are all right at home. Don't worry, I always look after myself.

6.1.47   Letter 5

Last day of my holiday and I go back to school tomorrow. What a day it's been too! The plumbers and joiners have been working in earnest and our house has been looking like something after a blitz. We have been in a mess. There have been men in the front bedroom, men in the back bedroom, one on step ladders in the kitchen, and even one on top of the stove, all banging, hammering and sawing. We're fairly tidy now, but if they go on at this rate it will soon be finished. They say we'll be able to have a bath by next week, although the rest of the work won't be finished.

I went to your mother's yesterday, and one of my letters to you only arrived there last week, so she's given it to me to post on to you. Last night we were wondering what you would be doing. Look after yourself, no matter what sort of place you are sent to.

Gosh, but it's cold here today. It's been snowing all day and it must be well below freezing. I hope we shan't be long without a fire when they start the fireplace. When I finish this letter I'll have to help to count coupons, not a job I like.

I'm wondering when I shall know your address again.

8.1.47   Letter 6

Our Peggy is the proud mother of quins! One died during the night, but the other four are going strong: two black and white and two white and black if you see what I mean. Poor Peggy was in agony last night, but is the proudest and happiest dog in the world tonight. Three of the pups are dogs and one is a bitch, and one is spoken for already. I'm thrilled to bits with them.

We've got our bath. It's not installed yet, but it's upstairs, and the lavatory and wash basin are upstairs too. We shall be without a fire on Friday, I believe, when they put the fireplace in.

School hasn't been too bad yet and it makes the days go quickly. About fifty of our girls are going to a camp school for three months at the end of January so our classes will be considerably smaller for a while. About eleven of my girls are going if they pass the medical exam.

You know, Ronnie, I even read about football in the papers when you aren't here to do it. Rochdale won 3-2 at York last Saturday.[111] Charlton lost at Manchester.

I think I'll have an early night tonight. But in spite of that my head is so full of plans for us. I'm thinking about furniture and such things. Please would you do something for me when you come home, if you can get the wood? I'd love some low bookcases. I think they'd look lovely beside the fireplace, and I really have a lot of books.[112]

10.1.47.

Here I am back at Villach. There are no Loyals left now. They sent us all back to this transit camp. I don't think I'll be posted to another regiment, so will probably stay here and do jobs in the camp.

It's now 2.30 p.m. Friday. I left the Loyals 7 o'clock Wednesday night, arrived here at 11 o'clock yesterday morning, all that time on a freezing train with no heat. It's colder than ever now, 27° below freezing.

I hadn't been in the camp five minutes when I had to take some prisoners to Klagenfurt and didn't get back until 11 o'clock last night. I was freezing. I pulled some floorboards up and made a fire. There will probably be nothing left of this hut by the time I've finished with it.

---

111 Ronnie was a lifelong supporter of Rochdale Football Club, and regularly went to watch matches when he was demobbed.

112 Ronnie was quite talented at carpentry, as well as drawing. He did eventually make the bookcase, together with several other household items such as a coffee table, a cutlery drawer, and a doll's bed for their daughter. Whatever he knew must have been learned from carpentry classes at school, since after the age of ten, he didn't have a father to show him how to do practical things.

I can't tell you how glad I'll be when this life is finished in the army. Since I left home I've been messed about all over the place. It's a good thing I haven't got long to do otherwise I'm sure I'd go crazy. At 3.15 this afternoon I take some more prisoners back to Klagenfurt. They come here every morning and return in the afternoon after working in the camp. It looks as though I'll be stuck with this job for a while.

They've just told me not to put any address because they don't know which part of the camp I'll stay in. I should know in my next letter.

10.1.47 Letter 7

I think there will soon be a letter for me from you at Villach. You're going to have a lovely collection of letters by the time I know your address. This will be the seventh.

I'm just listening to a lovely little piece of piano music as I write this: Sheep May Safely Graze *by Bach. I used to play it as a piano duet with my music teacher. She was always very nice. Now the radio programme has changed to Eric Barker in* Merry-go-round *with the double-or-quits quiz at the end.*

This is my third "stay in" night. I've even resumed my knitting, and can say that there are great hopes that it may be finished by the time you see me again. After all, I've only been at it for five months!

You know what one of those silly workmen has done, put his leg through the floor upstairs while the floorboards were up and there's a beautiful big hole in the shop ceiling now.

We've got orders for at least three of Peggy's pups now.

Time does seem to have gone queer. It seems like yesterday since you came on leave, and years since you went back. That was the best surprise I ever had in my life, coming home and finding you here like that.

Goodnight, be happy. Make the best of your life out there.

12.1.47.

Once again I've just arrived back from Klagenfurt at 11 o'clock on Sunday night. I can hardly see to write this as the light is so bad.

It's still terribly cold and snowing. I've never seen the army in such a state as it is today. There are hundreds of troops leaving this camp going to the Far East, battalions breaking up left and right, blokes being sent to units which no longer exist: what a mix up.

Every day I think, well, Hilda will be getting up now, combing her hair, having a bath, going to school, coming home, in bed; I just couldn't think about you more.

12.1.47   Letter 8

This is probably the last time I'll be sitting by this old fireplace to write to you. I believe it really is going tomorrow.

Last night I went by myself to the Rialto to see Concerto. *I enjoyed the music in it, Rachmaninov's Second Piano Concerto, but I didn't enjoy being alone.*

Pop left £1 in his overall pocket at work. He didn't like to tell my mother about it because he might have had it stolen, so unknown to her he's gone down to Whittle's tonight to get it.

We've got a new kind of bus ticket on our route now. They're the kind like they have at Blackpool, where the tickets are thin and come out of the machine like toilet paper.

PS Pop has just come back. He hadn't left £1, he'd left £2 and a packet of Woodbines there.[113]

---

113 Wilfred smoked unfiltered cigarettes heavily; most of the brands are no longer available, e.g. the Woodbines mentioned, Players Navy Cut, Craven A and Wills Whiffs.

14.1.47.

I've just been in the office to find out about the address. I've played hell with them. I've told them if I don't get it within the next couple of days I'll go and see the CO.

I've not drawn any pay since I came back. There's very little to spend your money on; spent about £1 since I left home on cigarettes, tobacco, tea and cakes. There's a small cinema in this camp, two films a week, months old. I either saw them at home or in Graz. As I told you before, there's nothing in Villach except a NAAFI and bombed buildings, so you can imagine what the place and life is like here.

Still snowing but much warmer which makes life a bit more bearable.

I've been with a staff sergeant most of the time here. I knew him in the Loyals. He is in charge of the maintenance of weapons. He's a very nice bloke, lives in Tottenham. He's twenty-three years of age, married with a baby girl fifteen months old. We keep looking at each other's photographs. He's been here nine days waiting for a truck to take him ten miles from this camp to some workshops.

I read today's paper and noticed there's nothing but strikes again in Blighty. It makes my blood boil. They should put them in the army. They'd soon change their minds. What a state the world is in: the papers are full of strikes, riots, political differences. I've done nearly five years in the army helping to prevent all this but it's worse than ever. The British Government is hopeless, far too easy-going, and where steps should be taken to remedy things they are never done. Out in Palestine now troops are still getting killed. The five years I've given the army are just wasted. Why are English people just like sheep? I won't talk about it any more, it makes me mad.

I've been very busy today, acting as camp sergeant major, bawling over the microphone to get blokes on parade going to Blighty and others going to Italy. It's now 4.15 p.m., in five minutes I'm going for my tea and then I have to take the prisoners back to Klagenfurt. It's usually between 10 and 11 o'clock at night when I get back.

14.1.47   Letter 9

I've had two of your letters from Austria now, one from Villach and one from Graz. Even though I can't send my letters on yet, all this time I've been thinking of you.

I'm sorry it's so cold. If only I could be there to keep you warm.

They haven't put the new fireplace in yet. They were going to put it in yesterday. Now it's going to be tomorrow and we've had the carpet up two days in readiness. However, they've put the bath (with black sides), wash basin and lavatory in, and hot and cold taps in the kitchen, even though we haven't got the water yet.

When I was coming home on the bus yesterday I had a feeling that something was wrong, and when I arrived home it certainly was. The electricity was off. Mother was looking for candles, there was a burst in front of the shop and all the water was going in the cellar, and we had no water from the taps. I rang the waterworks and they sent someone to fix the burst, and Mrs Owen lent some water. This is anything but home sweet home at present.

What a dreadful journey you've had! Wherever you are posted, let's hope it isn't a bad journey.

I suppose you know that Rochdale lost at Charlton on Saturday 3-1, but to console you I heard someone on the bus today say they played a fine game.

17.1.47.

I've been told not to put any address yet. It's hard enough being away from you but not being able to hear from you makes it 1,000 times worse. This afternoon I was thinking how nice it would be if I were going to school to meet you, to go and have tea together, perhaps to go to the pictures or dancing. Life is glorious when we plan things together, with your bedroom as our little home. I'm even looking forward to working in your father's hen pen![114]

17.1.47   Letter 10

We've got our new fireplace in and it looks lovely. We've got hot water in the kitchen now (from a tap as well as the geyser) but we can't have a bath or use the upstairs lavatory or wash basin yet because they haven't fixed the drains.

Of course the decorating has to be done yet and the new wall put in upstairs, but we can see how it's going to turn out.

It's lovely and warm with the new fire. I was going to write last night but when I came back from modern dance, the house was such a mess that I just had to tidy things up. Annie and Auntie Emily have been here helping this afternoon.

Marjorie thinks she will get married in June. She's got her first lot of furniture points and dockets. How I wish I knew exactly when we were going to get married.

---

114 Hilda's father rented a dilapidated barn and a small piece of land from the farmer just a few yards behind the shop. He kept hens there, meaning that the family had had fresh eggs all through the war.

18.1.47   Letter 11

Saturday night, and I'm spending an evening by the new fire, mending stockings. It seems to have been a long day: I even have to get up early on Saturdays now with the plumbers here. It's been mainly a day of housework for me. I persuaded the surveyor Mr Oldham to let us have the kitchen wall altered so that we can have the stove there, it looks so out of place where it is.

Cuddles and Lucifer are just having one of those all-in wrestling bouts now. The day when the fire was out Cuddles climbed right up the chimney. Silly little cat. Peggy's pups are like little puddings, they are so fat and cute, and just starting to open their eyes. You can always rest assured that there are plenty of animals here to look after me. Or maybe it's the other way about.

19.1.47.

I'm writing this in the sergeants' mess, which is about the warmest place in the camp. It's 3 o'clock Sunday afternoon and in half an hour I take the prisoners back to Klagenfurt. They finish earlier on Sundays.

Everyone in the camp has a terrible cold and I feel as though I've no life left in me. My head is in a whirl, my throat is sore, I can't sleep at nights. No wonder, everything is so damp and miserable in this camp. I wouldn't mind if I knew something definite, but a day here seems like a month.

Roy the staff sergeant left here the other day, which didn't help to make things brighter. Now I sleep in the room alone, I can't even have a fire now because we've burnt all the floorboards.

20.1.47   Letter 12

So you've ended up in Villach after all, and in 27° of frost. Soon I'll be
able to send you all my letters: I hope you won't have been too lonely
without them. It hasn't been so bad for me, being able to receive your
letters and know you are well. I don't know how you stand it in that
climate, so cold, and having to burn your floorboards too.

It had demob dates in the paper yesterday and your group 49 is
due for release April 28th to May 24th, which is just about what you
thought it would be. That's not too bad, is it?

I've nearly finished my jumper now. I'm on the last sleeve, then
I've only got to sew it up and it's done. I'm going to do some ironing
now, but things could be worse.

21.1.47.

I went to see about my "Python"[115] today and was told I'll
definitely be going on it in February, so it's only a matter of
about three weeks and I'll be home.

They told me not to put any address on my letters because by
the time you receive this letter and by the time I get a reply from
you there would only be a few days left before I came home. If
you've written any letters, save them for me until I come home.

Wouldn't it be wonderful? I should get twenty-eight days'
leave which will finish sometime in March. That means I'll only
have about a month to do before I'm demobbed. It couldn't
work out better. I seem to have been away from you ages; not
being able to hear from you makes the time seem longer.

I went to the pictures in the camp last night, two films on the
same programme. I hadn't seen them before, the Marx Brothers

---

115 "Python" was the general code name for leave given to troops who had
done four years or more abroad and were due for home posting.

in *A Night in Casablanca* and Burt Lancaster in *The Killers*. I enjoyed them. It made a change from looking at the camp.

I was very busy this morning washing my clothes, and I tore up some floorboards from another room to make a fire and boil the water. The fire didn't last long. It's been so cold today that when I felt the clothes this afternoon they were frozen stiff.

In ten minutes I take the prisoners to Klagenfurt, and when I get back I've got to make out a nominal roll of the men going on tomorrow's train to the UK, about 400 of them.

22.1.47 Letter 13

I'm writing this at school in my free period, having marked a set of geography books, and, of course, having acquired some entirely original ideas on the geography of the USA.

I'm going into Manchester after school to book seats for Annie and me at the Opera House to see Romany Love. *It's a bit of a trail, but the only way of being sure of seats.*

Our bath at home isn't workable yet as they haven't finished the drains, but it ought to be any day now. We are having to wait for plasterboards before they can put the partition up. And our fireplace, well, we're all in love with it.

I seem to have been back at school ages but it's only a fortnight. I suppose you feel like that too. I do wish I could send all my letters on. I've even bought sixteen stamps in readiness, though I believe this letter is number thirteen.

By the way, you still have your camera, haven't you? Because I believe it's quite easy to get 35mm films if it's that type. Think of all the fun we're going to have making our own story in pictures. And I wonder how many Williams juniors we're going to have the pleasure of photographing? I'd like to make a complete story of his (her or their) life in snapshots.

23.1.47   Letter 14

Another letter from you today, the third this week, and still I can't post my letters.

I agree with you. It does seem, with all the strikes and all the unrest in the world, that the years you have given to the army have been wasted. But maybe there is a purpose behind it somewhere. Maybe we'll know it years and years ahead even if it does seem a little hard now. I can thank God that you will be coming home in one piece.

I've had the first bath in the new bath, last night. But the workmen hadn't fixed the window properly so there was an icy draught from it. I had to make it a short bath or I'd have been frozen. It's better now though, and we can use the upstairs lavatory too! It's sheer luxury, even if it still isn't partitioned off from the bedroom.

I'm glad you've had somebody decent to keep you company and that you don't have to queue for your meals.

How long does it take you to get to Klagenfurt? It seems to be a long journey every night for you. Do you go by lorry? Pick a safe driver if you do.

24.1.47.

I've just arrived back from Graz, where I went last Wednesday night, and it's now 11 o'clock Friday night. Two wicked nights I spent on the train, no heat, 28° below freezing. Honestly, I didn't know I had any hands or feet. I must've walked miles up and down the corridor to try to keep warm. My reason for going was to take two British soldiers there for a court martial, escorted by six men.

One of them received the death sentence for murdering an old woman in Vienna. She found him drunk so took him into her house and gave him what food she had. Certainly, she didn't deserve murdering for that.

The other bloke received a life sentence for shooting an Austrian civilian in the face with a Tommy gun which killed him instantly, and then he threw him off the train, so you can imagine it's not been a very nice two days.

First thing I did when I got in the camp was to tear some more floorboards up and make a roaring fire. What a wonderful thing a fire is when you're cold.

There's only about two weeks to go before I come home and it's so hard to wait. They can't send me on "Python" yet because you've got to be back from leave for six weeks. Officially my leave finished on the 22nd December. They don't know I had the extra days; only you and I know that. Anyway, we'll just have to wait and see.

25.1.47   Letter 15

I'm simply bursting with things to tell you. I do wish they would let you have your address soon.

Firstly, the most important news. We may be able to get married sooner than we thought without having to wait for Marjorie to get married first. You see, one of my mother's houses is likely to come empty soon, the one next door but two.[116] My mother says if it comes empty we can have it if we wanted. What do you think about it? It's only small so it wouldn't need much furniture – one up, one down and a kitchen, but it's in good condition and clean. She says we could have a modern fireplace put in and come here for our baths. I'm sure you'll agree to this. It's all so difficult when you aren't receiving my letters yet, but I think you'll approve if I take the responsibility on my own shoulders, and tell her we'll have it if it comes vacant. Then I

---

116 This is the cottage at 424 Halifax Road, which Ronnie and Hilda did move into, and live in for seven years.

could start cleaning it and decorating it, have the fireplace put in and start collecting things for it before you're demobbed. Then we'd be well on the way to having a home. And if you got that job in Australia, we shouldn't have a terrific amount of possessions to dispose of with it being a small house.

Actually, I think it would really be better than having my bedroom here, firstly because we shouldn't have to wait so long for it, and secondly it would be more private. And the rent would be ridiculously small, 5s. 6d a week. You could almost call it living rent-free. Tell me as soon as you can whether you approve or not. I do hope you will.

As a matter of fact, the story of how it will probably become vacant is rather a sad one. A single woman has been living there – a very clean woman – but lately she's been ill. They found out she had cancer in her breast, as well as something wrong with her leg, so a week ago they moved her up to her sister's. Since then she's been dangerously ill. It's unlikely that she will recover, otherwise I wouldn't have told you all this about the house. I feel terribly sorry for the woman, and really I would rather she had been well, even though it meant no chance of the house for us. But this is what annoys me: yesterday, the rumour got around that she was dead, and believe it or not, ten people came to see if they could have the house. Vultures! As far as I know she is still alive, and I'm glad she is. But it just shows you what people are like.

I'm looking after the shop by myself tonight. Pop has gone with Whittle's men to the football match at Preston against Barnsley. I see Preston won 6-0. And afterwards they were going on to Blackpool, so he won't be back until 11 o'clock. I've let my mother go out, and of course Marjorie is out with Tom so here I am, just me and Peggy, the pups and the cats. The pups have grown terribly fast: they are only two and a half weeks old and yet they've had a go at lapping milk today. We have lots of laughs at them, waddling around. I'd love to photograph them. That reminds me, I've got you a 35mm film for your camera.

27.1.47.

I'm still at Villach.

Twenty-five blokes awaiting posting in this camp had been here for six days, last week they all went absent and are now classed as deserters as they are still absent. I honestly feel like deserting myself but I realise it's never worth it. The atmosphere of the camp is horrible, seeing the same old things day in day out, same sort of food every day. It seems to go colder instead of warmer, everybody's burning wood out of the huts, about fifty per cent of the huts in the camp are caving in. It's just like a skating rink wherever you walk and everything is so damp.

I think every letter I sent you since I've been in this camp has been full of grumbles but I know you'll forgive me.

I'm hoping with all my heart that this time next week I'll only have a day or two left before I'll be coming home. I haven't slept well at all in this camp, firstly because it's so cold, and secondly because I just lie there thinking of you.

27.1.47   Letter 16

I'm so sorry for you being without fire. I do hope they move you soon from that horrible camp, and that your cold is better.

About this house, if we get it, really it ought to be lived in because the council has powers to requisition houses that aren't being lived in. Do you think there is any chance of you being able to get a special licence before leaving Austria if you get your Python leave? If you came on leave and we didn't have a licence, we should have to wait until the banns had been called three times before we could get married. I do wish I could post this to you immediately to let you know all about this and to know what you think about it.

It's a world full of snow here at present. It hasn't really stopped snowing for a few days. I bet it's deep in the morning.

Our puppies are the loveliest things you could ever hope to see. They have started to lap milk and they are even cutting tiny little teeth.

Great progress with our bathroom. They've just started to put the partition up, and tomorrow they are going to alter the kitchen so we can have the stove there.

Let me know when, how and where you think we ought to be married. Thank you for writing so often, without any letters from me.

30.1.47   Letter 17

It's terribly cold here now. The newspapers call it Arctic weather. I've never known anything like it. People think of nothing else but keeping warm. The streets were almost deserted. One place in Gloucestershire has had 32° of frost. But at least we have not got down to burning our floorboards yet.

I'm going to have a nice hot bath tonight. It's lovely not to have to go down in the cellar for it.

I bought two saucepans today, pale blue enamel. I'll have quite a collection of odds and ends in a bit. I love buying and planning things for others. You should just see our house now. We've had the wall into the kitchen knocked down ready for extending it and what really made me laugh was that my mother had the door there closed, although the wall has gone, to stop the draught![117]

I don't like to think of you out there in this cold with no letters from home. It can't be long that we have to wait, and we have so many hopes to keep us going. As long as we have each other it will not be such a bad old world.

---

117 In real terms, the kitchen was never extended. This was just a matter of reallocating space in the room behind the shop so that the scullery became very slightly larger, thus reducing the living space.

Ronnie did get his lengthy "Python" leave at this point, and was not sent back abroad again. The letters resume just over a month later. Since after his leave he was posted in Preston not too far from Rochdale, from March until he was demobbed in May he was able to come home for at least a day every weekend. So Hilda and Ronnie saw each other every few days during that time, but still carried on writing to one another during the week. Ronnie is clearly becoming increasingly frustrated at not being demobbed, and at not having anything really worthwhile to do.

Sgt. R.H. Williams

Depot The Loyal Regiment

Fulwood Barracks

Preston

5.3.47.

I had to take my crown down after all[118], but can wear it when not in the barracks as I've still retained the rank of staff sergeant. However, I've just put sergeant on my address.

---

118 That is, the crowns sewn onto each arm of his uniform jacket indicating that he was a staff sergeant rather than just a sergeant. For some reason, the move back to Britain again seems to have made a difference to existing ranks.

I arrived in camp at 9 o'clock last night but by the time I'd got some blankets and found somewhere to sleep it was 10.30. I went in this office today and they gave me a job of taking some prisoners to and from the cookhouse. What a boring job. It lasted until 5 o'clock tonight, then at 6.30 we had a mess meeting which lasted until 7.45. Since then I've had a shave and whitened my belt. I've left a white belt at home. I must have that for the wedding. Oh, and I used your sweet little iron to press my pants; it's wonderful.

I suppose I'll just do odd jobs until I get demobbed, however I'll let you know from day to day what I've been doing. By the way, 49 group has been speeded up a bit. I shall now be out any time between April 22nd and May 5th, so seven weeks should see me home for good.

The prospects of weekends home seem very bad so far. I've heard you're only allowed one forty-eight-hour pass a month, and also one thirty-six-hour one. I will let you know as soon as I can. I'll ring you up on Friday night at 7 o'clock.[119]

I haven't been warm since I left home. It's freezing in these barracks, with no fires or anything to keep us warm. My hands are terribly cold.[120] I sleep in a great big room with three more sergeants whom I knew with the Loyals in Austria. The food is okay but not enough, so they've gone into Preston to buy some food which costs them about 4s. each in a cafe as there is no NAAFI. We can only get forty cigarettes a week.

I'd sooner be a soldier abroad any day, but not since I met you. Just think, you should get this letter by tomorrow night, I can ring you up and I can come home to see you.

---

119 The "leave" situation turned out to be not as bad as Ronnie originally thought.

120 The winter of 1947, starting in January, was believed to be the snowiest one since the mid-nineteenth century. According to the records, snow fell every day somewhere in the UK for a run of fifty-five days, and some drifts did not melt until the summer.

6.3.47.

Your letter came this afternoon, and I shall be waiting for your phone call tomorrow at 7. Just think, I got your letter less than a day after you'd written it. It's wonderful.

It doesn't really matter about you not having to wear your crowns, does it? It's not so bad even if you do only get one thirty-six-hour and one forty-eight-hour leave a month: that's only until April, and I can come and see you either for my holidays or during them or both. It's so different with you being in England where we don't have to measure distances in thousands of miles.

Our house is lovely and clean now.

There was a real row at home this morning. Pop versus Marjorie. She snapped at him as usual after he'd cooked her breakfast so he asked why the hell she couldn't speak properly and there was a bit of an argument in which he told her that she'd have to be different or look for somewhere else to go before her wedding. I believe she was as nice as ninepence when she came in at teatime. She must have realised that nobody else would have her.[121]

I pulled my shoulder a bit at modern dance tonight, nothing much, it just hurts a tiny bit and you know what? There were five blackjacks[122] in the changing room! One even got in a woman's bag which was on the floor. I might tell you I was up on a form at the first mention of them, horrible things!

10.3.47.

What a lovely weekend it was with you at home. It makes everything so different when I know that I can see you often. Did you have a good journey back?

---

121 The situation must have got bad, because Wilfred was the kindest, nicest and calmest person imaginable.
122 Large black beetles.

I finished reading Hiroshima *on the bus last night, and I still wasn't sick, though there was one page I had to skip.*

There are yowls of misery going on. Cuddles has just been smacked for pinching potted meat.

It's a nasty dampish, coldish, slushy, sleety day here today. I should say it's thawing at the rate of about 1° a week.

Don't forget about the Royal.[123] You know, I can just see us there. And you do look nice in your new suit.

10.3.47.

10.30 p.m. Monday. I'm tired tonight, being on my feet all day at the court martial and didn't finish until 9 p.m.

I had a game of billiards, or rather snooker, tonight, and I won, so you can tell how bad the other bloke was.

I don't know what I'll be doing tomorrow, probably getting blokes to shift snow. It's about eight inches deep on the barrack square. It's much colder here than in Rochdale, probably because the barracks are so open. There is no coal at all now except for the cookhouse and for a very small fire in the sergeants' mess where I'm writing this. I should be coming home this weekend, however I'll be able to let you know better when I ring you up on Friday. What a difference to travelling all those miles; your life was always at stake abroad.

12.3.47.

This will be a short letter because lights out is in ten minutes. I've only just come from Blackburn where I had been with six blokes on a burial party. It was for some old man who used to

---

123 The Royal Hotel on the esplanade at Cleveleys, where they did eventually spend a week.

be in the Loyals. It was a cold job, snowing and a terrific wind blowing. I'm so cold now. It's murder in these barracks without fire; they should shut the place down until there's some coal.

By the way I've put in for a forty-eight-hour pass for this weekend. If I get it I'll be home about 9 o'clock Friday night, but be at the telephone at 7 o'clock in any case because I may not get it. I'll ring you up if I don't. If I do get home at 9 o'clock on Friday I'll come straight to your house.

12.3.47.

Your letter came this afternoon. When you ring me up on Friday I want you to tell me if there is a good train through from Preston to Manchester on Saturday because I want to go shopping in Manchester on Saturday morning and I could meet you in Manchester then. We could stay in Manchester for the afternoon or come back to Rochdale, just as you like. You see, I'm assuming that you will be coming.

It's a wicked night here – blowing a real blizzard – just as bad as ever it's been these last two months. I bet the roads will be bad tomorrow.

17.3.47.

I shall have to write this in very small writing as I've only got this piece of paper left and no one seems to have any. I'm writing this in my room in front of a small fire. I managed to pinch some coal from the officers' mess. It's been a terribly boring day, just walking round and getting blokes to clean round the camp.

The sergeants have a dance tonight. I think I'm about the only one who hasn't gone. If I go to a dance it will only be with you. Usually these army dances end up in some sort of a brawl – they go for the drink rather than the dancing. The sergeant I told you about who sleeps in this room has gone to the dance. He was drunk when I came back on Sunday. I believe he'd been with some prostitute in Preston. A married man too, he surprised me. Of course you find people out as you live with them. I can't understand people being like that.

Thanks once again for a beautiful weekend. Even if we didn't go out it was wonderful. I'll read your book sometime this week. Thank you for the cake, and the chocolate which I ate this morning. I'll be thinking of you tomorrow night at the whist drive with your mother and Thursday night at dancing class.

17.3.47.

I've been thinking about this weekend. Even though we didn't go out it was worthwhile, wasn't it? Last night I tidied up my bedroom and the room looks really lovely by lamplight. I'm sure you'll like it. We could get our curtain material with the dockets, couldn't we? What colour do you think would be best? And you think we could get some bedding? How many blankets have you?

You won't have to stay in next Saturday because I've booked for the Rialto, second house.

Tonight after tea I went with Marjorie to see Mr Bates, the vicar, about her wedding banns. She's having them called out in April. She chose her hymns and all that. Are there any hymns or music you like particularly? I told Mr Bates I'd be going to see him soon with you. I was asking him all sorts of questions about which side to walk up the aisle and all that. I got him really mixed up, and he had to find a magazine with some wedding photographs in before he could tell me. There are all sorts of questions: father's name, father's occupation… The banns should be called out simultaneously in the two parishes – and there would have to be a certificate from your vicar saying that they'd been called.

We had no heat on in school today. There was no coke.

I've been practising whist at school today, but I lost. I shall hardly have the nerve to play in the whist drive.

19.3.47.

I smiled when I received a parcel from Mother yesterday. In it was some salt, tomatoes, two hard-boiled eggs, bread and butter, cake and some fruit. Wasn't it nice of her to send it? All because she thought I might be hungry. Although she could do with it herself I soon got stuck into it.[124]

I'll be very happy when this next month is over and I'm away from this camp. What a waste of time it is. Of course this is only one camp out of hundreds where men are wasting time waiting for demob and yet people talk about manpower shortage.

20.3.47.

I got your letter yesterday, the same day as you posted it. I didn't write back last night because it was the whist drive, you know. Don't laugh at me, but I won a prize – the consolation prize! I did have some awful cards, I really did. You should have seen the look on my mother's face when she knew I'd won the booby prize. I suppose that's what you call "beginner's luck".

When I got off the bus today in Rochdale I met Annie looking for my mother and Auntie Emily so I joined her and we found them in the Carlton. They've got chips in the Carlton again! That's great news. After tea I went up to Annie's. I tried her wedding dress on and I think it's going to be all right.[125] We're going to have the neck and sleeves altered a bit. I think you'll like it, but you won't see it until the wedding day.

---

124 Ronnie's mother and sister Hettie were still terribly poor.
125 Hilda did borrow Annie's dress for the wedding.

I didn't tell you what I won as my prize last night. It was a box of powder and a blue powderpuff – not bad really, almost worth losing for, in fact.

Don't forget to write to the Royal – though I can tell you roughly what the terms are now because I saw it in the Manchester Guardian *– 8 to 11 guineas per week.*

At the beginning of the Easter holidays Annie and I are going to have a real shopping day in Manchester catching the 7.30 bus so we can get some good shoes when the shops open. My mother bought a blue two-piece for the wedding today, quite posh I believe. I haven't seen it yet as it's being altered.

24.3.47.

Thank you for a lovely weekend.

I lost at cards today. It's certainly a good job we don't play for money!

There's bags of preparation at school now for the dancing competition I'm organising next Friday. We'll be having dancing all afternoon.

I wrote to Mash last night and asked her amongst other things if she'd be able to get to our wedding on June 24th.[126] I have to ask some people even if I know they can't come.

26.3.47.

Thank you for another lovely letter which I received this morning. Even though I've seen you at weekends I still look forward to a letter just as much as ever.

---

126 In fact in the end the wedding was on June 21st, a Saturday. It is striking that, unlike most weddings today, which are planned a long time in advance, less than three months before the ceremony they still did not have a definite date, the honeymoon destination had not been decided when Ronnie was demobbed in May with just a few weeks to go, and most of their furniture was not bought until they came back from their honeymoon. This was not a matter of choice, but of necessity based on availability.

I went to the pictures last night to see *The Laughing Lady*, not bad. Tonight I pressed my pants with your little iron, then played snooker in the mess, won two games, lost one; definitely improving.

I shall probably be home Friday night but if not I'll meet you in Manchester on Saturday at ten to four.

By the way, I've spent 3s. today on potato crisps, eighteen bags at 2d each. The whole lot wouldn't equal one potato![127]

26.3.47.

Only two or three more days before I see you again. The weeks seem to fly by. Before we know where we are, I shall be walking up the aisle to you. I've been reading the marriage ceremony in the prayer book tonight, just to get the general idea of things: "with my body I thee worship", and all that. There's something rather lovely about the words of the service.

---

127 A couple of short letters follow this one, in which nothing has changed in the situation, and Ronnie has no real news.

Ronnie must have had more leave at this point, and the final few letters are dated after a break of over two weeks.

14.4.47.

It seems such a long time since I last wrote to you: it must be over a fortnight now. But I've been seeing you, and that's better.

My mother is beginning to wake up to wedding details now — where we're having the reception, who is catering, which taxis and so on. We'll be getting things sorted out soon. We must go to see Mr Bates this weekend.

School wasn't too bad today, it passed quickly. Peggy's bridesmaid's dress is already made.

My mother met me in Rochdale today and I went with her for a fitting for her two-piece, and then I tried to get a hat. I didn't exactly get one, but I got a promise of one if I go on Friday after school and take my skirt with me so I can match the colours.

Which are you looking forward to most next weekend, dancing or the football match? As if I didn't know!

16.4.47.

What do you think of this awful Budget? No, don't tell me. I think I know. Cigarettes at 3s. 4d a packet! I'm cutting down somewhat drastically. Everybody at school is cutting down[128], and only one person has asked mother for cigarettes today, which is an all-time record. Pop is disgusted beyond words.

I haven't booked for the pictures yet because I don't think it will be hard to get in at Beau Geste.

All Marjorie's things are going tomorrow, and Marjorie herself departs in two weeks. And it's about nine weeks to our wedding.

16.4.47.

I won't be home Friday night because I'm on duty. I've tried to get out of it but I can't. If I come home I'll only get in trouble and it's not worth it with just over a fortnight to do. I'll try and get away sometime Saturday morning.

---

128 The cutting down did not last. Like her father before her, Hilda was a heavy smoker to the end of her life, and both of them suffered from health problems as a result. At the time, smoking was seen as something glamorous, and it was Hilda who encouraged Ronnie to start smoking. In later life he gave up, she refused even to consider it, and the matter became the subject of furious arguments. It seems extraordinary now that less than 20p a packet in today's money could be considered expensive. However, relatively speaking, the increase of 1s. on the price of a packet of cigarettes by the Chancellor of the Exchequer, Hugh Dalton, in the Budget in April 1947 was an enormous hike of over fifty per cent on top of the previous price. The objective of the increase was of course not to stop people smoking (bearing in mind for instance that soldiers were still being given a cigarette ration) but simply to generate more income for the Government.

21.4.47.

Another day nearer to being with you forever. Honestly, these last few weeks have seemed longer than the first five years' service in the army. I shouldn't grumble because I've been home most weekends since I've been here. In fact, I have everything to be thankful for.

21.4.47.

I've been to put the banns in. They're going to be called on Whit Sunday and the first two Sundays in June.

What a wind there is today. Somehow, I like these great big winds that come tearing in. They seem to blow everything unpleasant left by winter away. I remember when there were high winds at Scarborough and they blew the spray from the waves higher than houses and the waves were tremendous.

Mr Bates said that we could drink toasts if we had the reception at St John's.[129] I don't know what to do. He rather seemed to want us to have it there. I'll let my mother decide which place as she'll be paying for it. Are you particular about having it at the Egerton? Let me know if you are, before we make any arrangements. I can't make up my mind, but there's not much difference between the places, and the geyser at the Egerton is always breaking down.

---

129 They did have the reception in the church hall, known as the "Schoolroom", in the end. In fact, the room was scarcely ever used for teaching any more. The real school, St John's C of E Primary School, had been established in Victorian times, just yards away from the church. Hilda started teaching there in 1955, and although the school moved to a bigger building (a former secondary modern school in Wardle) in the mid-1960s, she carried on teaching at St John's until she retired in 1984. In her final term of teaching she was the acting deputy head, but she never got the promotion she deserved because, she felt, she was not a member of the Church of England.

You know what? Mr Bates uses the form of the marriage ceremony which doesn't make the bride promise to obey – just to love and cherish.

I've got my hat, I like it, I really do. And I got something else – an electric iron before the sixty-six and two thirds per cent tax goes on!

23.4.47.

Thank you for your beautiful letter. Even though I come home at weekends I look forward to a letter from you just as much as when I was abroad.

Thanks for putting the banns in. As you say, it's another step nearer. It doesn't matter where we have the reception, St John's, Egerton, anywhere, as long as we get married.

I'm trying to get home Friday night, but if I don't manage it I'll send you a telegram early Saturday morning telling you where to meet me.

Went to the pictures last night, Bette Davis in *Stolen Life*, quite good. That's it now until payday on Friday – I'm broke except for 5s.[130]

23.4.47.

I've only a few more letters to write to you while you're in the army. It will seem funny not to need to write any more. But I know what I'd rather be doing, writing or talking to you.

It's a wild night. I like the wind, but I don't much like the rain that comes with it.

---

130 Ronnie obviously had more things to spend his money on once he was back in England, not least travelling backwards and forwards between Preston and Rochdale.

I've bought an electric iron. I called for it today. I've had to borrow some money from my mother. Roll on payday. There are such a lot of things I want to be buying.

I've got four pillowcases, at least my mother got them for me today, really nice ones and only 3s. each. She also bought our wedding present for Marjorie, a lovely tablecloth – 37s. 6d.

I'm only buying necessary things, but gosh what money they take. If only you could win on Littlewoods or something like that.

Peggy came yesterday and she did enjoy her tea. Then we went to the Rialto to see School for Secrets *– very good too. Ralph Richardson is clever.*

I've issued a few invitations to those at school, and I think they'll come to our wedding. The list of invitations keeps growing.

28.4.47.

Well, I handed my kit in this morning, another step nearer. By the way, will you tell Marjorie I won't be at the wedding but that it wasn't without trying. They told me this morning I couldn't go until Saturday, either that or wait another month, and I couldn't stick another month of this.

I'll be thinking of you at the wedding but I'm hoping to be home Saturday night.

28.4.47.

What a weekend we had: I think we (or at least I) must have pre-wedding nerves.

I've been to see about a gas oven today. They are going to send the salesman up here. You see, they have to see that we really need one and have no alternative method of cooking.

Auntie Emily wasn't in last night so we went across to Bill's. You

194

know that chap Bill Fitton who goes there? Well, he knows the chap Lovick who has a furniture shop and he says that we might be able to get some furniture without units if we haven't enough. We might even be able to get a three-piece suite. You know I reckoned that furniture up wrong. I was thinking it was over £40 for a dining room suite but it isn't. That's for a settee, etc. The table, chairs, etc. are £20–£30, not much more than we'd pay for two easy chairs if we didn't get a three-piece.[131]

I can hardly believe that it's only a matter of days before you get demobbed now. I shan't have many more opportunities of writing letters to you now, but I must write this. Always remember, I love you with all my heart and my life would be empty without you. Whatever happens to us, whether we become rich or poor, adventurous or dull, happy or sad, whatever we become, to me you will always be my own Ronnie, my soldier that I fell in love with.

30.4.47.

The last letter I will write to you while in the army. Whether I'll ever have to write to you in civvy street neither of us knows. If ever I do I know it won't be like it's been in the army. By that I mean I'd only probably be away from you for a few days at the most.

To write letters, normally, that doesn't mean much but our letters have meant so much to each other. We've learned even to understand each other in them. From the time we met we had so little time to decide on things. We made the decision to get engaged, a decision I've never regretted, and never will.

---

131 They did get their furniture from Lovick's, and continued to buy things from there for many years. Their oak sideboard, still in use, was £18 16s. 9d, and the oak dining table, also still being used, was £9 13s. 3d. Their most expensive item of furniture was a three-piece suite which was £42 7s. 6d. All of this was bought on 2nd July 1947, after they came back from honeymoon. The total bill was £118 5s. 9d, and presumably the money came from Ronnie's army severance pay.

I've had nothing but happiness since I met you, you've been truly wonderful, the glorious things we've done together will live in my memory forever.

I shall never forget the first time I left you to go back off leave; those last few minutes, how precious they were. I missed you terribly. Every moment you were in my thoughts, every opportunity I had I wrote to you.

Then I came home on the course but I went straight home to see you, then went back to Austria. But then three weeks later we were together again at Filey, a heavenly week, one I could never forget. Just before that leave ended I had that terrible cold and you looked after me. You were wonderful.

Then I went back to Austria for the longest period I'd ever been away from you, five and a half months. A lifetime, or so it seemed, away from the one you love. It was agony, wasn't it?

Then home again when I had ten days longer than I should have had, all because I was in love with a very beautiful girl.

Back to Austria and five deadly weeks in Villach, then home again on Python, another thirty days of heaven even though the weather was lousy and your house was upside down. But those things didn't matter because I came home to be with you.

Then to Preston where I've been nine weeks and home at weekends, as well as six days' Easter leave.

I've a lot to be thankful for in so many ways because I've met you, been able to see you so much recently, and have come out of the army as I went in, in one piece. Shortly, we'll be starting a new life which I intend to make the best of for both of us and for our children. We are young and terribly in love, what better start could there be in our new life?

I suppose you wonder why I've written all about what we've done: well, it's one of my ways of trying to thank you for what you've done for me, for your love, your thoughts, your faith in me. Thank you for all the beautiful letters you sent me in the army. Some day we'll be reading these letters to each other.

Goodnight, my beloved Hilda, I'll be seeing you soon forever. My love is yours with all my heart.

God bless, darling, always.

30.4.47.

So this is it at last, my last letter to you in the army. We little dreamed how long it would be before I could write this, but now at last it's here, and we are about to start our lives together.

Thank you for everything you've done for me in the seventeen months since we met, for being so sweet, for putting up with all my whims and tantrums, and for loving me.

I seem to be striking rather a serious note tonight, but then it is serious, this business of starting a new life, for that's what it will be. I wonder how we'll get on, adapting ourselves to each other's personality? I suppose there must be a lot of give and take about it to make a success of marriage.

I'll try, darling, I promise you I'll try very hard. Be patient with me if I'm not perfect all at once, because if I go on loving you I can't go far wrong and I shall go on loving you, and having faith and trust in you as long as I live.

There's something magical about love that I don't ever want to lose. I can't explain it. Maybe it's a look in your eyes, or a beat of my heart; sometimes it's a kiss, sometimes a word or two but it's magic.

Don't let's ever lose it. If we do we'll have lost something absolutely irreplaceable. Don't let's get so concerned over wedding details, furniture, money and the like that we forget the thing that started it all, our love.

I remember all the sweet little things you've done for me, the parcels you sent to me, the letters you've written. We've a wonderful life in front of us. I'd like to be able to remind myself of that every time some little things go wrong. Let's not get in a rut. Let's always keep a sort of feeling of adventure about things, looking forward to the unexpected, never letting it take us by surprise.

I wonder if historians will ever condescend to look back to this post-war period, and feel a scrap of pity for those like us – no war – but no peace – with half the things we need obtainable, and the other half on dockets, coupons or units, or else too highly priced to be bought. It's a mess of a world at the moment. But I'll be darned if we'll ever need the UNO to settle disputes for us at 424 Halifax Road. We'll fight them out ourselves, and then kiss and make up. You see, I'm making allowances for our all too human failings. But that doesn't mean to say that we shan't be happy, in fact, as far as I'm concerned, we'll have a darn good try at it.

Was there ever a letter written with so little news in it? But then, today's news is tomorrow's history, and I'm feeling by no means historical. I'm just a girl who is looking forward more than she can say to having her man home for good, a girl whose idea of heaven is to be able to walk down the street with her man by her side, to be able to look at him and think: "He won't go away anymore. I'm very, very happy".

Good night, Ronnie my darling. God bless you. I love you very much.

The Wedding

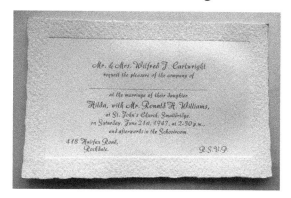

The wedding invitation.

Utility furniture buying permit, issued before the wedding.

Hilda's engagement and wedding rings. Worn for the rest of Hilda's life from 1947 onwards, the engagement ring is now so thin it is almost at breaking point.

Wilfred and Hilda about to enter the church, with the Schoolroom, where the reception was held, in the background.

A proud Wilfred and radiant Hilda about to walk up the aisle.

*Edith at the wedding, wearing what we know
from the letters was a blue suit.*

*From left to right, Bill, the best man, Ronnie, Hilda's cousin Jack
from Birmingham representing the Cartwright family (he was the
son of one of Wilfred's sisters who survived to adulthood), and a
friend of Ronnie's.*

Ethel and Hettie at the wedding.

The bridesmaids: on the left, Susan, Bill's daughter, in the middle, Peggy Jamieson, Hilda's fellow teacher and friend who was the matron of honour, and on the right Valerie, Marjorie's daughter.

Bill's wife Annie, his mother Emily, who was Edith's sister, and Emily's husband Jess.

Les and Enid, Hilda's girlhood friend from the Guides who sang at the wedding, and Marjorie and Tom: two more couples who married in 1947, the former in October, the latter on 3rd May. Hilda was a bridesmaid for Marjorie.

Ronnie's army jacket, in which he got married.

Hilda's cousin Alice, daughter of Edith's brother Willie who had been killed in the First World War.

Ronnie and Hilda's wedding certificate. Despite their
extraordinary maturity, when they married he was just twenty-
three and she was twenty-two.

Ronnie and Hilda at the
church porch after the ceremony.

Ronnie outside St John's
Church after the ceremony.

Humorous McGill postcard sent by Hilda from Cleveleys to her parents, whilst she and Ronnie were on their honeymoon. Even something so light-hearted contained an exhortation on the back to continue to save money, even though the war had been won.

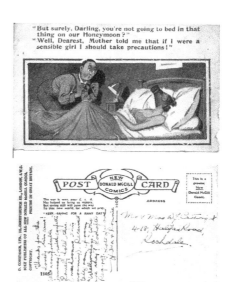

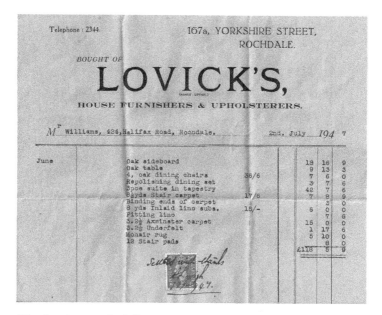

The furniture which Ronnie and Hilda bought from Lovick's in Rochdale on their return from their honeymoon.

EPILOGUE

Ronnie and Hilda got married on a sunny Saturday, 21st June 1947. By modern standards everything was arranged at the last minute: even a few weeks before the ceremony they still did not know where they would have the reception, attended by about fifty people, or where they would go on honeymoon. These proved to be respectively the Schoolroom of the church, and the Royal Hotel on the esplanade at Cleveleys. Wilfred walked proudly down the aisle to give Hilda away, Hilda's friend Enid, whom she had known in the Guides, sang, and Ronnie gave a speech at the reception which surprised people by its eloquence. The picture of them cutting the cake was so striking that the photographers, Allen Handley, kept it on display in their shop window for months afterwards to entice other young couples to use their services. Certainly, Enid and her fiancé Les had their wedding photographs taken by the same company. Also, a friend of Ronnie's, with whom he had lost touch, walked past and saw the photograph one day, and went in to ask where he could find Ronnie, and so the friends were reunited.

After coming back from their honeymoon, and only then getting most of their furniture, they moved into Hilda's parents' cottage at 424 Halifax Road, where they would stay for the next seven years.

Anyone who reads this story must be wondering: "But did the marriage last?" Yes it did, remarkably, considering that Ronnie and Hilda had got engaged after knowing each other for an astonishingly short time. They had their ups and downs and arguments over the years, as all normal couples do, but if things went wrong, they made up and carried on. They knew each other for sixty years, were married for fifty-eight and a half of those, and were separated only by death, the death of Hilda, as it happened.

They were never apart again for more than a few days, except for one academic term in the 1970s when Hilda went to do an education course in Exeter, and even then Ronnie visited her there.

For the rest of her life, Hilda provided Ronnie with the stability and affection he had always craved. He was asked repeatedly if he was going to stay on in the army, even by a lieutenant-general, with almost certain prospects of very rapid promotion. Although he was a model soldier, like all the young men of his generation, he had had absolutely no choice about being conscripted; now he had served his time, he had lost five years of his youth under the most dreadful circumstances, and all he wanted was to get home and get married. He was given a marvellous reference when he left the army, saying that his military conduct was "exemplary", and a testimonial which read: "Smart, clean, well turned out. Good disciplinarian and honest. Thoroughly trustworthy and reliable soldier. I can thoroughly recommend him to any employer".

Ronnie did go back to his old job at Thomas Robinson's, where there were no prospects of promotion, but with Hilda's teacher's salary they got by, and had quite a carefree time in the first few years of their married life, socialising and playing a lot of sport together, such as tennis and badminton. Also, Ronnie was a very fast runner: he won prizes regularly in his company's annual sports day; he cycled to work; he was always extremely fit.

It was only in 1953, when Hilda was expecting Wendy, their only child, that it became apparent that the one-up one-down cottage where they lived would no longer be big enough for them, and in August 1954 they were allocated a three-bedroom council house in Ashbrook Crescent, on a small development off Halifax Road, and within five minutes' walking distance from the shop at 418. The house was in fact one of the new buildings erected in 1947, when the building trade gradually took off again, so it was only a few years old when they moved in.

They had an indoor bathroom, but otherwise the house was in the style of an earlier generation, with a coal fire in the lounge and in two of the bedrooms (although the bedroom fires were never lit unless someone was really ill), and with a coke stove in the kitchen. The real parquet floor downstairs was attractive, the metal window frames not so much so. In very cold weather the difference in temperature between indoors and outdoors would regularly make the window panes crack with a big bang.

Ronnie decorated the entire house, and created an attractive garden where there had been a wilderness. They were still very much lacking in modern conveniences, e.g. still no television, no fridge and no telephone: they would not have those luxuries for another few years – but they were happy. Ronnie got his first car, a black Morris Minor, in 1959. He passed his driving test after only a handful of lessons, perhaps because he had already been used to driving trucks and tanks in the army.

Hilda went back to work full-time, after having worked briefly part-time, when Wendy was eighteen months old, leaving Wendy with her grandparents in the shop during the day. When Wendy was four years old, she started school at St John's C of E School where Hilda was teaching by then, next to the church where Hilda and Ronnie got married, and a few doors down from the shop.

They stayed in the council house, clearly with more responsibilities than previously, until 1967, when the family moved into a house with Edith, again on Halifax Road but further towards Littleborough than the shop, at Hurstead.

During these years, Hilda and Ronnie continued to have a good social life, taking full advantage of their spare time in the evenings. They would sometimes go out to the pub, Ronnie played for Smallbridge Badminton Club, and when he grew older he took up crown green bowling. Very much as in her unmarried days, Hilda went to evening classes such as continental cookery (despite having said in her letters that she felt she could learn to cook just by reading the recipes!). She was always willing to try new types of food, and enjoyed Indian, Chinese and Italian cuisine. Despite all his years abroad, Ronnie never took to any kind of foreign dishes, and at best grew to like pizza. Hilda also went to German classes and bridge classes, eventually joining a local bridge club.

She had to some extent regretted the fact that she had gone to college rather than university, but made up for that by doing an Open University degree which she completed gradually over several years, mainly in education and history of art. She graduated in the early 1980s, and the graduation ceremony was held in Preston.

Like most people from the 1960s onwards, they had foreign holidays, in France and Belgium for instance, and in Italy, which Ronnie continued to love all his life. He never forgot the kindness and generosity shown to him by the Italian people during the war, when they had so little themselves.

Wendy's parents gave her the great gift of a good education: like Hilda, she went to Bury Grammar School, in 1964, and was then the first person in the family to go to university. In that same year, after so much time, Ronnie finally acknowledged that he would never make any progress at Thomas Robinson's; he was still only earning £10 a week. He handed in his notice and took another job as an office manager for more money, but what he gained financially he lost in stability. Over the following twelve years or so he would be made redundant four times. He hated desperately being out of work and would do absolutely anything to earn a bit of money until he got a proper job again. All his life, self-respect meant everything to him. On one occasion, for some time when he was out of work, he would go across the road to the paper shop at 5 o'clock every morning to sort out the papers ready for delivery, just to hold on to his dignity by earning a bit of cash.

It was only in his last few years of work that he got the job he liked best of all, working as an inspector for the rates office of Rochdale Borough Council. It meant he had to be out and about for much of the day, inspecting properties and checking that they were in the right rates band, and it also involved talking to people a lot, which he loved. Ronnie was always gregarious, often unstoppable once he started talking, and he had a real gift for getting people's life stories out of them within a matter of minutes, not because he was being nosy, but because he was genuinely interested in them.

Hilda retired shortly before her sixtieth birthday, a few weeks before the birth of her only grandchild, meaning that she was able to give occasional help to Wendy, who by then lived in Nottingham. Ronnie carried on working until he was sixty-five, and the time came to make a major decision. Although they had lived on or near Halifax Road all their married lives, because the family was so small, it made sense for Ronnie and Hilda to move to be near Wendy, where she was bringing up her son Simon as a single parent. It was felt that they would still be young enough to make new friends and carry on their usual activities, and this proved to be the case.

In fact, in 1989, Hilda and Ronnie moved into Wendy's house in Nottingham, and she and her son moved into a slightly larger house round the corner, since she was by then self-employed, working from home, and needed a room to use as an office. When they had settled in, Ronnie and Hilda did establish a new social life. Hilda joined the local bridge club and went to Italian evening classes, and Ronnie joined an ex-servicemen's association, the Fellowship of the Services, eventually becoming the president of the local group. They would also go to the local pub, as well as going on outings and on holiday with Wendy and Simon, or taking Simon on his own.

In the next few years, throughout Simon's primary school days, they were a tremendous help in looking after him. They would collect him from school and give him his evening meal, play with him, and it was Ronnie who taught him how to play cricket and football. Hilda helped him to learn to read and write, and was delighted when, at the age of five, he started to learn to play the piano, using her piano bought for her in her own school days.

However, from the mid-1990s onwards, Hilda's health began to deteriorate. The boot was on the other foot, and Wendy helped to look after her for several years. Although Hilda had never been in hospital in her life until her seventies, not even for Wendy's birth, which had been under the care of a midwife, her stays there started to happen all too often. She had trouble with mobility, and had one hip replacement, but was never fit enough to have the other one done. Because she had smoked heavily for so long, she suffered from breathing difficulties, and in the last year or so of her life she had macular degeneration, and her sight began to fail. She could no longer read novels, and could barely even watch the television.

Her end, when it came, was very quick. She was admitted to hospital the morning of one day, when Simon had just come home from university for Christmas, and died in the evening of the next. It was as if she had been waiting for him. Wendy was with her, holding her hand, when she died on 12th December 2005, aged eighty-one; Ronnie had left the hospital only minutes before. The causes of her death were recorded as primarily old age, but also acute renal failure, chronic obstructive airways disease, and congestive cardiac failure.

Her funeral was conducted by a Methodist minister at the local crematorium on a beautiful crisp snowy day, and her ashes were scattered there by Ronnie, Wendy and her son, a few days later. Although there was space in Ronnie's parents' grave in Rochdale, she would not have wanted to be buried there, since she never knew Ronnie's father, and was never close to his mother. She has an entry in the Book of Remembrance which can be seen every year on 4th August, her birthday.

It goes without saying that Ronnie was bereft and terribly lonely when Hilda had gone; Wendy visited him every day, but a daughter is no substitute for a wife. Sometimes he was overcome with grief, sometimes he was angry with Hilda for leaving him, thinking that if she had taken better care of herself, she might well have been with him for longer.

He was finding it increasingly difficult to get up and down the narrow stairs at home, and, ever a pragmatist, he agreed that it would be better to sell his terraced house and move to a small flat in a nearby sheltered housing association development with a warden employed there. Within a few months he had moved, but was only a few doors away from where Wendy lived, and she could go in and make his evening meal every day, and he had many kinds of other help to enable him to maintain his independence. At least there, he had people to talk to.

Ronnie lived on for just over ten years after Hilda died, and despite his loneliness, and despite countless operations, he always retained some quality of life, right until his very last day. During those years, Wendy saw him almost every day (the rare times she did not, someone else would take her place), and got to know him better than she had ever done before. He had never before admitted, for instance, that his family had once been evicted for not paying the rent, because he felt it was so shameful. It was also obvious that, because Hilda had enjoyed a better education, he had always thought she was intellectually superior to him, and Wendy pointed out that intelligence and education are entirely different things: Ronnie was in fact very clever and resourceful, and at least Hilda's equal in most things. On the subject of education, he lived long enough to see Simon gain many academic qualifications, get a very good job, and be happily married to Katya.

Ronnie was an extraordinarily brave man. He could make a fuss about things that didn't matter, but when it came to something important, he was always, all his life, a real fighter. Starting in the 1980s, these are just some of the medical problems he had: firstly, a mild heart attack, after which he stopped smoking immediately; three hip replacements (one of the operations went wrong because of a faulty design of the prosthesis); two cataract operations, one of which also went badly and had to be corrected by laser treatment; an operation to repair a perforated ulcer, which very nearly killed him, only days after one of his hip operations; an operation on a hernia in his groin; an operation to remove a damaged disc from his back; fitting of a pacemaker; several minor strokes and an operation to clear his carotid artery to stop him having further strokes; and crippling arthritis, which meant that he virtually lost the use of his left hand. He also had type II diabetes.

After each episode he would be slightly further diminished, but would still soldier on. Until he was eighty-eight, he still achieved plenty and got fun out of life, although he gradually became increasingly less mobile. Wendy took him out for meals and brought him home regularly. He joined the national Italy Star Association 1943-45, for veterans of the Italian Campaign during the war, and managed to go once to their annual reunion in Chichester. With the help of friends, and by taking flights from the local airport, even though it meant getting him onto the plane in a special lift, over a period of several years he was able to go to Jersey, Guernsey, Cornwall, and even, for the very last time, for a short trip to Italy, where he enjoyed a glorious day on the beach in Viareggio, categorically refusing to take shelter from the sun.

Everything changed drastically for the worse in late 2011. Ronnie had two falls in one day in his little flat, and although he was not badly hurt, he was taken to hospital for observation. Whilst he was in hospital, his mobility deteriorated drastically. He was sent to a rehabilitation hospital, where he remained for several weeks. When he went there, he could still walk a few steps, with difficulty, but then he caught a chest infection and became so weak that he lost the ability to walk at all. The realisation that this was the case was heartbreaking for someone who had once been so fit, but the only complaint he ever made was: "Things are not looking very good for me…"

As Christmas that year approached, it became apparent that he would never be well enough to return to his flat, and Wendy had to find him a place in a care home, with only a few days' notice. Fortunately, she was able to get him a room in a home directly across the road from where she lived, but the downside was that almost all the residents had dementia, and Ronnie's mind was still quite sharp.

From then onwards, he had to be moved from his bed, to his chair, to his wheelchair by two carers using a hoist. However, once he was in his wheelchair it was possible for Wendy or Grahame next door, who was an extraordinary help, always, in Ronnie's declining years, to bring him home for meals or to take him out locally. On Ronnie's behalf, Wendy bought a wheelchair-adapted car which Grahame drove. Ronnie was still able to watch the television, he read the newspaper every day, and had his own telephone installed so he could still talk to his friends, including his best friend Alan who lived in Canada.

After two years, a brand-new care home opened, still within walking distance, and Ronnie moved there for the last two years of his life. Wendy still went in every day to make his evening meal, or, the rare times she could not go, Grahame would go on her behalf. A pub/restaurant, a little cafe, plenty of shops, the doctor and the dentist were all within pushing distance.

At least in this new home Ronnie was in beautifully furnished surroundings, and had more people he could talk to, although nothing could compensate for the fact that he had to ask for help if even the slightest thing was out of his reach. Most of the carers meant well, but they did not always have the time, experience or competence to cater for his needs.

The care was, of course, also extremely expensive. Hilda always used to say to Wendy: "At least I'll be leaving you the house," but that proved not to be the case. She and her parents would have been horrified to know that the four years Ronnie spent in care homes used up almost the entire value of their house, and had wiped out the very hard-earned savings from two whole generations.

Ronnie was becoming increasingly frail, and in the last week of January 2016 he seemed quite chesty. The GP was called to the care home, but said that Ronnie just had a cold and did not prescribe anything, although Wendy had said the previous evening that she thought he had a chest infection and needed antibiotics. He did not seem well for the next few days, but Grahame was still able to bring him in the wheelchair-converted car to her house for a meal on Sunday 31st January. Fortunately, he had the best evening he could possibly have had – he had one of his favourite meals of salmon, he watched a programme by David Attenborough, whom he admired immensely, and exclaimed in wonder at views of huge shoals of fish, saying, "Oh, just look at that!", he talked to Wendy and Grahame, and it was only when it was time for him to go home that he started to deteriorate suddenly.

The next morning, the care home called Wendy to say that he was really not well and that they had called for an ambulance. She was waiting for him in the late morning at the hospital when he got there, and he was clearly in a very bad way. Still lying on a trolley, he was given a drip, antibiotics and treatment for his diabetes: the doctors thought he might have pneumonia.

By the early afternoon, the treatment seemed to be working partially, and he rallied to the extent that he was even joking with the doctors. But then, from mid-afternoon onwards, he declined rapidly, his breathing became very laboured, and the doctors announced that he was not likely to last the night.

Although Ronnie had not heard this announcement, he realised he was dying, but was still not ready to give up the fight. Almost with his last breath he said repeatedly: "This is not going to happen, this is not going to happen". At least, thankfully, he and Wendy had time to say everything they wanted to each other. In the early evening, by the time it became possible for Simon to talk to him on a mobile phone, Ronnie could no longer speak, and could only nod. In the last hour of his life, by then in a coma, Ronnie was transferred to the dignity of a real bed in a side ward, and died at 10 p.m., only a few hours after being admitted to hospital, with Wendy holding his hand.

It transpired that the cause of his death was in fact sepsis, the cure for which can be antibiotics, if given soon enough. We will never know whether he would have lived for a little longer if he had been given antibiotics a few days previously, but what is certain is that no one would have wanted him to go on until he had no dignity and no quality of life left. He was an extraordinarily brave man, all his life, and he died as he lived: fighting.

Ronnie had a very dignified, high-Anglican funeral at Saint Mary's Church in Nottingham city centre, on 16th February 2016, which would have been his ninety-second birthday. It was the most appropriate of locations: Ronnie used to go to the Remembrance and Christmas services there when he still could, and Simon had been an organist there before and after becoming a cathedral and university organ scholar. Although Ronnie had outlived most of his friends, touchingly, people who had not seen him for quite some time turned up at the church. The fact that he showed such genuine interest in others had always made him popular.

Then, that year, on a beautiful hot day in July, just the sort of weather Ronnie always loved, and with a committal by the vicar of Rochdale Parish Church, Ronnie's ashes were buried in a casket under the new gravestone of his parents' grave in Rochdale Cemetery.

And so, they were both finally gone, leaving Wendy with an unfillable void, but profoundly grateful for all the years that she had had with them.

At the interment of Ronnie's ashes in Rochdale, the vicar asked: "What kind of person was he?" How can Ronnie and Hilda be summarised? Their bodies may have aged, but their characters were largely already formed when they first met in 1945. For the rest of his life, Ronnie retained his love of order and smartness, and he could not abide slovenliness, lateness or laziness. It was not just that he did not tolerate fools gladly, he would not tolerate them at all. If he called someone stupid they would laugh, thinking it was a joke, but actually he meant it! He could make the most outrageous comments, never hesitating to tell people what he thought of them, but because there was no malice in him, they usually did not resent it.

By the end of Ronnie's army career when he was twenty-three, he had witnessed and experienced more trauma than most people will ever know in a lifetime, but by contrast, in terms of romance, he was altogether innocent, and was completely, genuinely, knocked off his feet by what he considered to be his luck in meeting Hilda. All his life, despite all his emphasis on discipline, so necessary for his survival until his early twenties, he was a very kind-hearted, generous and loving person, and was never afraid to show his emotions. His interest in military matters continued into old age as he joined firstly the Fellowship of the Services and then the Italy Star Association, and when he could no longer take part in sport himself, he would watch it on the television, often for hours at a time.

Both he and Hilda were well-matched in being spontaneous and mercurial: Hilda's mother had warned Ronnie from the outset that Hilda "had a temper on her". Hilda did, as she admitted herself, like to have her own way, but if they had an argument they would make it up.

Despite the fact that Hilda was already well-educated when she met Ronnie, she never lost her desire for self-improvement with her evening classes and Open University degree. She had a genuine love of learning.

Despite their different backgrounds, Hilda and Ronnie had a great deal in common. They were both outgoing, fun-loving and gregarious, and loved going to dances and giving parties for quite a few years after they were married. Again this was nothing new; before Ronnie was demobbed, for instance, Hilda could not wait to find out whether he would get leave in time to go to the police ball.

Hilda loved sport as much as Ronnie did, although she gave it up sooner than he did. It must have come as a shock to them to have a daughter who was pathologically shy when young, hated parties and was completely useless at sport!

It is also apparent from the letters that neither of them was very much good with money. Although they were meant to be saving up for their wedding, Hilda talks about getting another dress, Ronnie says he would pay anything to buy her a new coat, and sends her parcels of expensive stockings. They were lucky in that they never had to get a mortgage; they lived for a peppercorn rent for several years in Hilda's parents' cottage, then they moved to a council house where they paid a low rent, and eventually they moved into a house owned by Edith, which they inherited when she died. In general though, they were prone to making some bad decisions about finances, for example they carried on renting televisions for years after everyone else had bought one because they were no longer likely to break down so much, and for several years had cars on long-term hire agreements, meaning that at the end of the contract they had to hand the car back, and never owned it.

They were not perfect; who is? Yet there was a great deal of good in them both. When they wrote their letters, they were an ordinary young couple making their way in extraordinary times, and this is their story, set down for posterity. Hilda wondered what history would make of them, and that is for the reader to decide. But for as long as someone reads about them and the tribulations and triumphs of their early life together, something of them will live on.

Their Later Life

Edith, Wilfred, Hilda and Ronnie sitting on the wall outside the shop, around 1950, photograph by Bill.

Wilfred and Peggy, early 1950s.

*A very natural family group, taken by Bill in 1957. At the back
Hilda, Wendy, Ronnie, Jess, Annie, Wilfred, and Annie's sister,
Grace. In the middle Susan, Emily, Edith and Marjorie, and at the
front Annie and Bill's twins, Jennifer and Christopher.*

*1959: Wendy and Ronnie at
Whitsuntide, which was always a
very dressed-up occasion.*

*The day of Edith's funeral in July
1979. At the back Annie, Wendy
and Charlie, Wilfred's youngest
brother, in the middle Hilda and
cousin Alice, at the front Hilda's
cousin Marjorie.*

Hilda's graduation from the Open University in Preston, in the early 1980s.

Ronnie, Wendy and Hilda during Hilda's last Christmas in 2004. Hilda and Ronnie were both eighty at the time; she died on 12th December the following year.

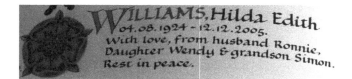

Hilda's entry in the Book of Remembrance at Wilford Hill Crematorium in Nottingham.

Ronnie aged eighty-six, on holiday in Cornwall.

IN LOVING MEMORY OF
**THOMAS HENRY
WILLIAMS**
1863 - 10.01.1935
AND HIS WIFE
ETHEL
28.08.1890 - 16.11.1963
ALSO THEIR SON
RONALD HENRY
16.02.1924 - 01.02.2016
WHOSE ASHES ARE INTERRED HERE
AND THEIR DAUGHTER
HETTIE
17.02.1923 - 27.02.1998

*Ronnie's new family gravestone in Rochdale, on the day of the
interment of his ashes in July 2016.*

APPENDICES

What Happened To...?

It would be good to think that everyone referred to in the letters had a happy ending. Unfortunately, that was not the case for many of them.

ETHEL AND HETTIE

Ronnie's mother Ethel must have hoped when he was demobbed that he would be able to help her with practical matters, as well as financially, but the fact that he got married almost immediately meant that he was never in a position to do much for her, and she and Hettie continued to live in very run-down rented accommodation, moving in the 1950s from Redcross Street North to a similar terraced house in Watmough Street. As she got older, Ethel suffered from crippling arthritis. She had to move her bed downstairs, could barely walk (of course there were no hip replacement operations then), and was constantly in agony. She died in hospital on 16th November 1965 of myocardial infarction, certainly embittered by the hard life she had led, going right back to 1929. Since that year, she had known nothing but loneliness and poverty, and, in her final years, also pain.

It might have been some slight consolation had she only known that at last her artistic talents have been acknowledged: some of her architectural drawings of Rochdale Manor House have been donated to the local studies library in Rochdale, which accepted them gratefully as a valuable resource concerning a now demolished building which had been in the town centre. Perhaps more importantly, Ronnie's remains are buried together with those of his parents; she had to manage without him in life, but in death, after very many years, she has got him back.

After her mother's death, Hettie carried on working, but otherwise struggled greatly to cope. The street where she lived was demolished in the 1970s, and she was moved by the council to a block of high-rise flats in Rochdale. For her, that was disastrous. At least where she lived previously neighbours would keep an eye on her but she knew no one in her new neighbourhood. Over the next few years she had a number of falls and broken bones, and Ronnie worried greatly about her: the fact that he had a mild heart attack in the early 1980s was almost certainly because of the stress he was under.

Then, in the middle of one night, Hettie seemed to lose control completely and started shouting out of the window. This was something she had done aged eleven, when her parents had to leave her and ten-year-old Ronnie for a day. She was diagnosed with schizophrenia. No one really knew what to do with her and she ended up in an old people's home at the age of fifty-nine. With the regular care she received there, she lived on until 27th February 1998.

Hilda and Ronnie had moved to Nottingham in 1989, but went to visit her when they could. Her death certificate recorded the causes as senile myocardial degeneration, dementia, schizophrenia, epilepsy, and CVA (cardiovascular accident).

WILFRED AND EDITH

Wilfred and Edith sold the shop in 1960, and moved into a brand-new bungalow off Halifax Road, for what they hoped would be a happy, well-earned retirement. This was not to be. Wilfred was worn out by so many years of hard physical work, such as working in the bakery, serving in the shop, carrying crates of beer up and down from and to the cellar. Heavy smoking had also damaged his health, and for a long time he had had a dreadful strangulated hernia in his groin which he did not tell anyone about because he did not want to cause any trouble – that was so very typical of him.

He died on 4th September 1961, aged just sixty-five, only a few months after his retirement. Hilda doted on her father and was devastated; he was a truly kind and gentle man who never had a bad word to say for anybody. Edith never really recovered, and never had the real pleasure she should have had from her own retirement. She was clearly lonely, and in 1967 she, Hilda and Ronnie decided that Edith would sell the bungalow and everyone would move in together into an old house, partly Georgian, partly Victorian, and formerly the house of the assistant manager of the nearby Hurstead Mill where Edith had worked as a young girl.

In 1946 Ronnie had expressed his concerns about moving in with his parents-in-law, and in fact the move in 1967 did not work out particularly well. Ronnie and Hilda felt that having Edith living with them restricted their freedom to some extent, and the situation was not helped by the fact that, in her seventies, her own health deteriorated and possibly she had a very mild touch of dementia. She had become a shadow of the vibrant person who had done so much to help Hilda and Ronnie years before, and had looked after Wendy when she was young.

Edith had to have an eye removed because she had developed glaucoma, and spent the last eighteen months of her life in a nursing home. She died, aged eighty-two, on 14th July 1979. She left the house in Halifax Road to Hilda and Ronnie, and to Wendy she left £200, which is what she realised for the sale of the cottage at 424 Halifax Road in the 1960s: she thought she was leaving Wendy the price of a small house. In fact, when Edith died, Wendy was in Southern Italy, and the £200, even then, went almost entirely on buying a business-class flight ticket to Manchester to get back in time for the funeral. Forty years later, Wendy still misses her grandmother greatly, for all her loving kindness and selflessness during Wendy's upbringing.

Auntie Emily, Bill, Annie and Susan

In addition to Susan, Bill and Annie later had two other children, the twins Jennifer and Christopher. They also ran a grocer's shop for quite some time. Jess, the husband of Edith's elder sister Emily, who was Bill's father, died in the 1950s. At the end of her life Emily went to live with Bill and Annie, and again the outcome was not very positive: they felt that she interfered too much in their lives.

Emily died in the late 1960s, and, to everyone's shock, Bill only outlived her by a short time. He died of a heart attack in his fifties, leaving Annie a widow for many years until she eventually died of old age. As was the case when Wilfred died, Hilda was terribly upset at Bill's death. She had always been very fond of him. He was a few years older than her, and had always been her protector and friend, right from when she was a very little girl.

Susan became a teacher, and married a curate, who was also quite a well-known racing driver at the time!

Tom, Marjorie and Valerie

The marriage of Tom and Marjorie only lasted for a few years. During that time they had a daughter of their own, Pat, and Valerie came to live with them. When they got divorced, Valerie lived with Marjorie and Pat lived with Tom. Marjorie never remarried. Marjorie was a good, kind person, despite the many problems she faced in her life, and Hilda got on well with her again when they were no longer living together in too confined a space. Marjorie certainly never deserved the tragedies she suffered. She was always fond of Edith, and grateful to her. Occasionally they would go on holiday together, and Marjorie visited Edith regularly in her old age.

Valerie was a pretty girl, and clever – she eventually became a Sister in a hospital. She had two illegitimate children, one child when she was seventeen, which she gave up for adoption, and another when she was in her twenties, which she brought up herself. Her health was always fragile, and when Valerie was in her fifties, Marjorie found her dead in bed of a heart attack. It is horrendous that Marjorie had discovered both her mother and her daughter dead, many years apart, and she never fully got over the shock of Valerie's loss. She began to suffer from angina, and died in 1999.

ELIZA AND IRIS

Eliza's heart was always in Ludlow and she continued to return to the town with her daughter, Mabel, and granddaughter, Iris, for many years. She always rose early in the morning and remained quite active into her eighties. Possibly as a result of giving birth to fourteen children she suffered from a painful strangulated hernia which was never treated. She passed away on 1st December 1956, aged eighty-five. She was fondly remembered by all those who knew her.

Iris joined the General Electric Company (G.E.C.) in Witton, Birmingham in 1949. She was initially employed as a general clerk and then specialised as an accounts clerk. The 1950s were a very happy time for her – she enjoyed her work and made good friends with her colleagues, some of whom she is still in contact with. In 1952 she met her husband-to-be, Bill, while at the cinema. Iris gave up full-time work after her marriage in the 1960s. A year later she gave birth to her only child, Andrew. He graduated from Aston University in 1989 and worked in publishing in London for twenty-five years. Now approaching her mid-eighties, Iris is cared for by her son at her home in south Birmingham.

HILDA'S FRIENDS

Inevitably, once she was married, Hilda lost touch with some of her friends from college, as well as from Elm Street School when she moved and began to teach elsewhere. However, in the 1980s, some of her college friends started arranging an annual reunion in Scarborough, which she went to several times, accompanied by Ronnie, before most of the people attending became too infirm to travel.

THE PLACES

There will never again be a time when people need to write to exchange letters every couple of days as Ronnie and Hilda did when they first knew each other. Life has changed beyond measure since the immediate post-war period. For a generation used to mobile phones, computers and the Internet, it is strange, now, to consider a society where most people did not even have a telephone, calls had to be arranged in advance from one public call box to another, and you had to go via the operator at the telephone exchange to make the call.

Few had an indoor bathroom, there was no central heating, no double glazing, and ice would regularly form on the inside of the windows in winter. There would be a larder or a pantry for short-term storage of food. With no refrigerators, meat in particular needed to be bought for consumption the same day, or the next at the very latest. There were no fitted carpets; the norm was lino, and rugs which were often still handmade peg rugs. Clothes were recycled and passed down, home-knitted and handmade, and there was endless mending. Televisions continued to be phenomenally expensive, compared with income, for many years after the end of the war, as well as being unreliable and with a poor picture. We live now in a very, very different world.

Surprisingly, every building that Ronnie and Hilda lived in during their long marriage is still there: the cottage at 424 Halifax Road, the council house in Ashbrook Crescent, the house at 578 Halifax Road (the newer, Victorian part of which has been very sympathetically restored by the owners who have lived there since Ronnie and Hilda left), and their Victorian terraced house in Albany Road, Nottingham.

However, most other locations have not fared so well. St John's C of E School, where Hilda taught and which Wendy attended, moved to new premises in the 1960s and the original building, which would still have been perfectly serviceable for other purposes, was demolished. There is still an empty, grassed-over space where it stood. St John's Church, suffering from a declining congregation, was decommissioned a few years ago, and is now derelict.

Between 1945 and 1947, Rochdale had seven cinemas and Littleborough had two. They are all gone, although the former Regal is now the cleverly cinema-themed Regal Moon restaurant and pub.

With the exception of Lovick's furniture store, which is now in a new location, every enterprise in Rochdale which Hilda and Ronnie mentioned is now gone. Haworth's department store in the Esplanade in the very centre of Rochdale has closed and is boarded up. At the time when the letters were written, there were two main shopping streets, Yorkshire Street and Drake Street. Drake Street was at that time home to all the most refined shops; it is now very sadly run-down, although there are apparently plans to make improvements.

The Carlton restaurant, just off Drake Street, where Hilda and her family and Ronnie went, had silver-service waitresses who still wore black uniforms, white aprons and white caps. It has long since closed.

Other sadly missed places on Drake Street are Halfpenney's, and Diggle & Taylor's clothes shops, the Glove Shop, and Butterworth's jeweller's. Shorrock & Shorrock, the music shop where Hilda got her piano in 1936, has disappeared. Iveson's was quite a large and prestigious department store, which at one time controversially had tortoises and monkeys in the building to attract customers! Beswick's footwear had the monopoly in the town for good quality shoes, and in the 1950s had a machine which fascinated young customers: schoolchildren would have their feet X-rayed, and marvel at seeing their own bones. Clegg's next door was a high-quality bookseller's.

The sad fact is that retail habits were beginning to change, and in the future these independently-owned stores, most of which had been run by several generations of the same family, would not be able to face up to the competition from national, or even international chains selling the same products.

The shop at 418 Halifax Road is no longer a grocer's – for quite a few years now it has been a hairdresser's – but the building is still there. Wilfred and Edith were very lucky in the sense that they sold their shop in order to retire in 1960, just when the very first supermarkets were starting to appear. Theirs was a world away from giant retail parks and Internet shopping. In the twenty-four years that they owned their business they had little or no competition: it was literally a corner shop, and although it kept similar hours, it was never a convenience store. People went there because, quite simply, there was nowhere else to get their groceries.

In the period when Ronnie and Hilda wrote their letters, in a stretch of a few hundred yards along Halifax Road at Smallbridge, there was a fantastic range of independent shops. People would do their shopping on a day-to-day basis; any perishable foods were bought for use mostly on the same day. Apart from Wilfred and Edith's grocer's, there was another smaller grocery shop, which was not an off-licence. There were two greengrocer's, one of which was next door to their shop, and across the road was the fish and chip shop. There was a butcher's, and a hardware shop which also sold wallpaper to order, and a hairdresser's. For problems with health there were a doctor's, a chemist's and an optician's. The nearest dentist was just down the road in Littleborough. There were also numerous pubs. For most daily requirements there was no need to go even into Rochdale.

As Hilda's letters show, visits to shops further afield were almost always to buy things for special occasions, such as trips to Kendal Milne and John Lewis' department stores in Manchester. It is clear from what she says, however, that by 1946 journeys by train for civilians were relatively easy – and cheap. In the eighteen months covered by the letters, she went for various reasons to London, Manchester, Liverpool, Southport, Blackpool, Leeds, Scarborough and Filey, and to visit a friend in Yorkshire, covering distances that even by today's standards are impressive: every few weeks she was on the move. These were also the final years of the heyday of the railway network.

What They Watched

The period in which the letters were written was a glorious time for the cinema, a cheap means of escapism for everyone in hard times, not to mention a vivid way of keeping up with the news in days when there was no television. Usually with an "A" film and a "B" film in each session, an outing to the cinema was marvellous value, and there was plenty of choice.

Ronnie could obviously only very rarely see films except when he was home on leave, but Hilda went to see them on average once or twice a week, sometimes with one or both parents or other relatives, with friends, and sometimes on her own. There was no age divide: her middle-aged parents would also each go on their own if there was no one else available. It was also a classless pastime, enjoyed by rich and poor alike. According to an online site, Media Statistics[132], the national average price for a cinema ticket in 1946 was 1s. 5½d. In Rochdale, it would presumably have been less than that. In later years, Ronnie told how shocked he was at the high cinema ticket prices whenever he was posted for training and courses "down south".

The following is a list of just some of the films Hilda saw from December 1945 to April 1947 according to her diaries and the letters she wrote to Ronnie. Sometimes she just writes

132 www.terramedia.co.uk

"Went to cinema", without specifying the film. Only a couple of them are films seen by Ronnie abroad.

Unsurprisingly, the titles of the films indicate that quite a few of them were still on a wartime theme. Many have faded into obscurity, but some, such as *Brief Encounter*, became enduring classics. A good number of the actors mentioned, who were great stars at the time, are well-remembered even now, e.g. Bob Hope, Bing Crosby, George Formby, Stewart Granger, Boris Karloff, Joan Crawford, Bette Davis, Rex Harrison, Charles Laughton, the Marx Brothers, Burt Lancaster, Marlene Dietrich, John Mills, Michael Redgrave and Ralph Richardson, to mention just some of them.

DECEMBER 45
Princess and the Pirate – Bob Hope

JANUARY 46
Guest in the House – Ralph Bellamy
Brief Encounter – Celia Johnson, Trevor Howard
Dead of Night – Michael Redgrave
The Way to the Stars – Michael Redgrave, John Mills, Stanley Holloway

FEBRUARY 46
He Snoops to Conquer – George Formby
Waltz Time – Kay Kendall, Richard Tauber
And Then There Were None – Barry Fitzgerald, Walter Huston
God is My Co-Pilot – Raymond Massey
Johnny Frenchman – Tom Walls

MARCH 46
Escape in the Desert – Jean Sullivan, Philip Dorn
An Enemy of the People
A Thousand and One Nights – Cornel Wilde, Phil Silvers

Bewitched – Phyllis Thaxter, Edmund Gwenn

Journey Together – Richard Attenborough, Jack Watling, David Tomlinson

Along Came Jones – Gary Cooper

April 46

Valley of Decision – Greer Garson, Gregory Peck, Lionel Barrymore, Gladys Cooper

May 46

Caravan – Stewart Granger

The Corn is Green – Bette Davis

Forever in Love – John Garfield

June 46

Indiscretion

July 46

Shock – Vincent Price

Destry Rides Again – Marlene Dietrich

The Captive Heart – Michael Redgrave

Within These Walls – Thomas Mitchell, Mary Anderson

August 46

Bedlam – Boris Karloff

The Bells of St Mary's – Bing Crosby, Ingrid Bergman

September 46

Rhapsody in Blue – Robert Alda

Wanted for Murder – Eric Portman

Two Sisters from Brooklyn – June Allyson, Peter Lawford, Jimmy Durante

Mildred Pierce – Joan Crawford

October 46

The Strange Love of Martha Ivers – Barbara Stanwick

November 46

Anna and the King of Siam – Rex Harrison, Irene Dunne
Captain Kidd – Charles Laughton
Jesse James – Tyrone Power
Make Mine Music (Walt Disney) – Nelson Eddy, Dinah Shore,
    The Andrews Sisters
Johnny Angel – George Raft

December 46

State Fair – Dana Andrews

January 47

Blossoms in the Dust – Greer Garson, Walter Pidgeon
Concerto
Monsieur Beaucaire – Bob Hope
Mr Ace – George Raft
A Night in Casablanca – The Marx Brothers
The Killers – Burt Lancaster

March 47

The Laughing Lady – Anne Ziegler, Felix Aylmer

April 47

Stolen Life – Bette Davis
School for Secrets – Ralph Richardson

Hilda's Story,
Finished in October 1946

The Peculiar Story of Mr Bundle

Nobody actually saw it happen. One minute Mr William E. Bundle, bank manager, respectable and rotund citizen of Highford, was walking along Sacker Street, nodding to his many acquaintances, peering over the rims of his spectacles into the shop windows, pleasantly anticipating a leisured lunch at the club, followed by a game of chess with old Bingleswade, and the next moment he was dead; definitely, irrevocably dead, lying on the pavement, surrounded by a growing crowd of aghast spectators, from whose ranks the murmurs, 'Bundle, poor chap, always knew he had a weak heart', 'Good job he has no family to be told', and 'Poor old Bundle!', were sympathetically rising.

The trouble was, it happened so quickly that Bundle himself didn't know it had happened, and the immortal soul of William E. Bundle continued its amiable course down Sacker Street, feeling quite cut up when Smithies appeared not to notice him, and Tomkins positively stared right through him. However, Mr William E. Bundle, alive, had been of a philosophical turn of mind, so Mr William E. Bundle, deceased, did not let the incidents perturb him unduly, knowing that Smithies had a vile temper, arising from the most inconsiderate liver, and that Tomkins had an overdraft at the bank.

The only thing that really surprised Bundle was that his appetite, which a few moments ago had been keen, and worthy of a man of his ample proportions, seemed to have disappeared completely. "Must have been the porridge at breakfast," he ruminated. "Can't stand it really. Don't know why I eat it," and engrossed in these thoughts, the spirit of Bundle turned in at the club, failing to notice that Robinson, the doorman, had broken the habit of thirty years, standing by letting him pass unnoticed.

Really, thought Bundle, *I hardly feel as though I want any lunch at all. Maybe it won't do me any harm to miss it for once. I really do eat far too much*, upon which he entered the lounge, thereby saving himself the embarrassment of sitting ghostlike and unwaited upon at his usual table.

The ironical feature of the situation was that Bundle had been a lifelong unbeliever as far as ghosts were concerned, and if he had been told, considerably earlier in life, that one day his ghost would be sitting, invisible, inaudible and apparently unconcerned in his favourite armchair at the club, he would have advised his informer to visit a psychiatrist, or more probably, would have said, 'You've been overworking, old chap. Why don't you take a holiday? Marvellous what a fortnight of sea air will do for you when you begin to imagine things.'

And there he was, as ghostlike a ghost as had ever haunted its former premises.

For a few moments, he sat in rapt self-investigation of his loss of appetite. He didn't feel ill. No! Not ill. In fact he was feeling rather well, quite light and buoyant, and that peculiar feeling of giddiness which had worried him all morning had completely disappeared. The truth was that he didn't ever remember feeling quite so well. And yet he had no appetite at all. And it was most peculiar that he didn't even want to drink, or have his customary lunchtime cigar. Well! There was no use in worrying about it.

So sat Bundle, meditating upon his loss of appetite, and blissfully unaware of the disturbances centring around him in earthly and spiritual circles. To be more correct, the earthly disturbances were connected with the seemly disposal of Mr Bundle's body in Sacker Street, while in spiritual circles there was great consternation at the non-appearance of Mr Bundle's psyche in higher realms. It was unprecedented, and there was no agreement as to where the fault lay. The Department of Spiritual Transport was certain that it had received no notification about the removal of Bundle from Sacker Street, yet the Department of Spiritual Initiation and Enrolment asserted that the necessary forms had been made out in triplicate and forwarded to the proper quarters, and the duty angel had confirmed this by showing the record book which stated quite clearly that William E. Bundle, age fifty-four years, eleven months, two days, five hours, six minutes and two seconds, was to be transported on that day, June 23rd at 1.16 p.m., for spiritual enrolment. There was a regrettable lapse somewhere, but where, indeed? Needless to say there was a growing anxiety as to Bundle's present whereabouts, for the aforementioned departments were not omniscient, and it would be necessary to call upon the services of one of the most elevated rank – possibly even an archangel. And what indeed might Bundle be doing with his newly acquired spiritual powers and no knowledge of the rules and regulations, without even the regulation handbook to guide him? Little wonder that there was feverish activity up above.

Their fears would have been largely dispelled could they but have seen Bundle, engaged in the harmless occupation of sitting in his favourite chair, with the knowledge of his spiritual powers at zero level.

However, an unusual situation is bound to have unusual consequences, and when Bingleswade walked into the club lounge, fortified by a hearty lunch, and eased himself into the armchair next to Bundle, the situation definitely became rather puzzling to our aforementioned spirit. "Hello there, Bingle," was the greeting which unfortunately the latter could not hear. "Had a good lunch? Didn't have any myself. It's most unusual I know, but I've lost my appetite. All the same, I wouldn't mind starting that game of chess."

Bingleswade continued his contemplation of the ceiling with the profound and satisfied gaze of one who had eaten well and was now enjoying the meal in retrospection.

"Bingle, I say, Bingle!" shouted his deceased and invisible friend. "What is the matter with you? Can't you hear me? I say, old chap, you aren't ill, are you?"

Silence ensued from Bingleswade, together with an apparently even more profound contemplation of the ceiling.

Exasperated beyond all bounds, Bundle jumped to his feet, and was just preparing to deliver a harangue of selected if not select adjectives to the blissfully ignorant Bingleswade, when he was disturbed by an unusually loud chorus of cries from the other end of the room. Turning round, he saw that about ten people had congregated around Tomkins, who had previously passed him in the street. Apparently, Tomkins had just entered the room, and had something of a rather serious and important nature to communicate. Always curious, Bundle treated Bingleswade to a glare which would have annoyed that gentleman intensely could he but have seen it, and then went to find out what all the commotion was about. As he approached, he was surprised to hear his own name being mentioned in sympathetic undertones, and, wondering what on earth he could have done that was of such interest, he joined the group. One may imagine his amazement on learning that the cause of his fame was his death. "Yes," Tomkins was saying, "I know it was Bundle. There he was in Sacker Street, dead as a doornail. Must have been a heart attack, you know. He always had a weak heart. Poor Bundle."

Upon that a chorus of sympathetic murmurs arose. Bundle was stupefied. *The silly asses,* he thought. *The blithering silly asses. Here I am, standing next to them and they say I'm dead. What a fool that man Tomkins is,* and with the desire to let the rest of them know what a fool Tomkins was, he tapped that gentleman on the shoulder and grinned expectantly at the faces around him. Nothing happened. At first, Bundle thought that it was all one monstrous practical joke. He hastily consulted his memory. He had once slipped a very good replica of a spider into Tomkins' soup. It might be retribution for that. Or was it 1st April? No! It wasn't even April! Then what the devil was happening?

But for a very small detail, Bundle might have remained in doubt for some considerable time about his ghostliness. As Bundle was gazing up and down at Tomkins in deep disgust, he noticed that Tomkins was standing on his foot, or so it seemed. And yet he didn't feel a thing! Fascinated, he moved his foot about. Yes, he could move it about under Tomkins' foot. No, it was not moving under Tomkins' foot! It was moving through it. "Good Lord!" said Bundle to himself, "I'm a ghost!" And with that realisation, he wandered back to his armchair to think things over, noticing absent-mindedly that Bingleswade had now joined the group and was lending his genuine regrets to the confused sound of voices.

"Well!" said Bundle. "Well!" as he passed his hand over his brow, and for the moment could say no more. Metaphorically speaking, he was stunned.

It is not every man who finds himself a ghost in his own club, and it was this reflection that set Bundle on a chain of thoughts. *It's a bit of a shock to discover that I'm dead,* he reasoned, *but I can't really grumble. I've had a good life, my idea of a good life anyway. No family to mourn over me. I've made some good friends. Sorry to leave them of course, but it had to happen some day. I've not had any outstanding vices. Had my faults of course – bound to have them. But I don't think that I've ever done anyone a really bad turn.*

Well! I'll just have to wait and see what happens. Maybe they don't know where to send me.

At that moment, 'they' were still in a state of considerable confusion. After much consultation, the two departments concerned had decided to organise a search party. It was not an easy task for any such party, for Bundle, had he chosen, could have been anywhere with his newly acquired powers. Accordingly, a selected group of spirits, including two of Bundle's former acquaintances, had been sent out. "But," the duty angel sternly reminded them, "this will have to be put down in records. It may mean that some of you are put on less specialised work for a time if he isn't brought in soon." There were many prayers said for Bundle's safe spiritual journey that day. He would have been quite flattered if he had known.

The gentleman (or should we say 'ghost'?) in question was only just beginning to realise the advantages of his position. He had never been much of an eavesdropper, but now he found out that eavesdropping was thrust upon him, so to speak, for the topic of conversation in the lounge was 'Bundle'. He was really quite touched to see how much concern was being shown for him. "Never realised they thought so much about me," he ruminated, and he longed to go over to his friends, Bingleswade in particular, and say, 'I'm all right, old chap, really I am', but remembering his former efforts at conversation, he remained seated.

It is no exaggeration to say that presently, Bundle began to enjoy himself. There was Deacon, to whom he had not spoken for at least six months, saying how much he missed him, and Smythe, at whose home he had often dined, saying, "The wife will be upset. She always did like Bundle. I wish I hadn't refused to lend him my lawnmower last week."

"Yes, he always returned things promptly," interrupted another voice. "I remember when I lent him a book." And so it went on. The simple soul of Bundle delighted in these compliments. His friends, like himself, had never been apt to flatter or praise a man in his hearing. So it was a good thing to note that he had been appreciated after all.

Leaving Bundle to his meditations, let us follow for a moment the exploits of the heavenly search party. One was diligently scouring the forests of Central Africa, and found only one stray pygmy soul who had disobeyed the rules and returned to his native haunts to see what had happened to his favourite blowpipe. Another was exploring with great curiosity the streets of Montmartre. As he had been a teetotal Rechabite in life, great were his discoveries on the ways of man. Another, if the truth be known, was slightly lost in the maze of Hampton Court. Only Harris, old club friend of Bundle's, had a shrewd idea of where to find the errant spirit, and was moving at great speed towards Highford, and the club in particular.

Leaving Harris literally in mid-air, let us take one more look at the heavenly HQ from which he is speeding at a rate that would turn any jet-propelled plane green with envy. The duty angel is glancing through one of the massive volumes that encumber the office. Suddenly he stops. His expression is one of horror. He reads again. "No, this can't be true!" he says. "What a terrible mistake. I shall certainly lose my halo for this if he isn't stopped," and at a speed flagrantly in excess of that stated in rule 11, section 2 of the Heavenly Handbook, whizzes after Harris who is now hovering above the club. For this is what the unfortunate angel read. 'Attention of duty angel. Decease of William E. Bundle to be postponed for ten years. Signed, Archangel Commanding Spiritual Transport'.

Bundle's own impressions of the next few seconds were a little blurred. He wasn't really surprised to see Harris standing in front of him explaining that there had been a slip-up, that he should have been collected earlier, and that he was sure Bundle would like the club up there. By this time he wasn't even surprised to notice that nobody else in the lounge appeared to see or hear Harris. Indeed, he was now a little eager to start the journey. "Bit of an adventure this," he was remarking, when suddenly there was a blinding flash of light. There appeared to be a glorious person in shimmering white, wearing a halo that was slightly crooked, and agitatedly whispering to Harris.

"Sorry, Bundle," said Harris. "I'm afraid I'll have to leave you after all. You'll be all right now."

There came a moment of darkness and unconsciousness. It passed quickly. Bundle was rather afraid to open his eyes. "You'll be all right now," a pleasant voice was saying reassuringly. Slowly, timidly, he looked up. The hospital doctor was standing beside his bed, speaking to him. Next to him, stood a nurse in spotless, almost shimmering white.

"Am I dead?" faltered Bundle wonderingly.

"No – not dead," said the doctor. "You had a heart attack. You must rest now. Don't talk," and he walked away, a very puzzled man. Later he said to the nurse, "I would have staked my professional career on the fact that he was dead when they brought him in. It's the most peculiar case I've ever met." But, after all, this is the peculiar story of Mr Bundle.

As for Bundle, his adventures remained for him as a most unusual dream, as the duty angel had decreed they should. "But," he pondered thoughtfully, "I really must ask Smythe if he will lend me that lawnmower of his."

And, as a point of interest, Smythe did.

About the Author

Wendy Williams is a translator and reviser, with academic qualifications in foreign languages, literature, and translation. Originally from Rochdale in Lancashire, she now lives in the East Midlands. Reading, writing, and social and family history are amongst her great passions.